# SMALDONE

# SMALDONE

## THE UNTOLD STORY OF AN AMERICAN CRIME FAMILY

## DICK KRECK

FOREWORD BY CHUCK AND GENE SMALDONE

FULCRUM
GOLDEN, COLORADO

Library of Congress Cataloging-in-Publication Data
Kreck, Dick.
  Smaldone : the untold story of an American crime family / by Dick
Kreck.
    p. cm.
  Includes bibliographical references and index.
  ISBN 978-1-55591-718-0 (hardcover)
  1. Mafia--United States--Case studies. 2. Gangsters--United
States--Biography. 3. Criminals--United States--Biography. 4.
Organized crime--United States--Case studies. I. Title.
  HV6446.K74 2009
  364.1092'2788--dc22
                                        2008055423
ISBN 978-1-55591-706-7 (pbk.)


Printed in USA
0 9 8 7 6 5 4 3


Design by Jack Lenzo
Cover photo: Clyde Smaldone returned from federal prison in 1962
happy to be home. In his first newspaper interview, he said, "I've got
no animosity against anyone. It's all over now." © *The Denver Post*
Back cover photo: Clyde and Checkers Smaldone, 1953. © *The Denver Post*
Background texture, photos: © Sahua | Dreamstime.com
Background texture, sidebars: © Nejron | Dreamstime.com


Fulcrum Publishing
4690 Table Mountain Drive, Suite 100
Golden, Colorado 80403
800-992-2908 • 303-277-1623
www.fulcrumbooks.com

Unless otherwise credited, quotes from Clyde Smaldone are taken from tapes made with his son Gene Smaldone in 1992.

# CHARACTERS

**Leo Barnes**—Partner with "Smiling Charlie" Stephens in the Blakeland Inn restaurant/casino. An attempt to blow him up in his car in 1936 sent Clyde and Checkers Smaldone and Stephens to the state penitentiary in Cañon City for four years.

**Ronnie Bay**—Childhood friend of Clyde Smaldone's son Gene.

**Benny Binion**—Texas gambler who later owned Binion's Horseshoe Casino in Las Vegas.

**Charley Blanda**—Head of the Pueblo mob and an intimate of Clyde and Checkers Smaldone. He was godfather to Clyde's son Chuck.

**Mother Cabrini**—Educator and future Catholic saint who taught Clyde Smaldone as a child.

**Al Capone**—Famed Chicago mobster who helped Clyde Smaldone get established in bootlegging in the 1920s.

**Albert "Bert" Capra**—Clyde Smaldone's brother-in-law and partner in gambling enterprises.

**Sam Carlino**—Early-day racketeer in Pueblo who, with his brother, Pete, known as "the Al Capone of southern Colorado," ran the mob there until he was shot to death in May 1931. Pete was murdered four months later.

**Vincenzo James "Black Jim" Colletti**—Leader of the southern Colorado mob after the death of Charley Blanda. A member of the Mafia.

**Frank Curley**—Head of federal rationing for western states during World War II and a source for Clyde Smaldone's black market operations.

**John Danna**—One of four brothers—Tony, Pete, and Sam were the others—who fought the Carlino brothers for control of the Pueblo mob. All four were murdered between 1925 and 1930.

**Paul "The Harp" Enrichi**—Reputed enforcer for the Smaldone mob.

**Barry Fey**—Onetime music promoter in Denver, a close friend of Fat Paulie Villano, and, for a time, a major gambler.

**Judy Good**—Girlfriend and wife of Young Eugene Smaldone. A racing-dog owner and drug user.

**John C. Jenkins Jr.**—Mayor of Central City who struck a deal with the Smaldones to run gambling in the mountain town during the opera season in the late 1940s.

**Judge W. Lee Knous**—Federal judge who sentenced Clyde and Checkers Smaldone to twelve-year terms in federal prison for jury tampering.

**John "Skip" LaGuardia**—Owner of the Alpine Inn in North Denver who challenged the Smaldones' gambling empire.

**Carlos Marcello**—Powerful New Orleans mob boss and a close friend of Clyde Smaldone.

**Frank "Blackie" Mazza**—A member of the Smaldone mob and a close family friend.

**Jerry Middleton**—Self-styled "Barber to the Stars" and a bookmaker.

**Gerald Nevins**—Companion and bootlegging partner of Clyde Smaldone during Prohibition.

**Judge Willis W. Ritter**—Federal judge whose bizarre behavior and extreme sentences got him removed from the Smaldones' jury-tampering case.

**Robin "Walkie-Talkie" Roberts**—Young gambler whose loose lips led to his death.

**Joe Roma**—Known as Little Caesar, he headed the Denver rackets until he was shot to death in his North Denver living room in 1933.

**Joe "The Ram" Salardino**—Associate of the Smaldones who, with his brother, Gus, ran gambling in Cañon City, Colorado.

**Anthony Smaldone**—Smaldone brother who operated Gaetano's, the family's North Denver restaurant.

**Charles "Chuck" Smaldone**—Clyde Smaldone's younger son.

**Clarence "Chauncey" Smaldone**—Youngest Smaldone brother, who, with his nephew Paul Villano, succeeded Clyde Smaldone in running the family's gambling and loan-sharking operations.

**Clyde Smaldone**—Titular head of the Smaldone crime family from the 1930s until he retired in the 1960s.

**Eugene "Checkers" Smaldone**—Gambler, bookmaker, and loan shark. Regarded as the toughest of the Smaldone brothers.

**Eugene "Gene" Smaldone**—Clyde Smaldone's older son.

**Jeannie Reeb Smaldone**—Chauncey Smaldone's second wife. Blamed by the family for causing dissension among the brothers.

**Louis Smaldone**—Son of Smaldone cousin Fiore. Briefly involved in the family's slot machine operations.

**Pauline Blasi Smaldone**—Chauncey Smaldone's first wife. She became involved in bookmaking.

**Raffaele "Ralph" Smaldone**—A North Denver grocer, small-time bootlegger, and father of the six Smaldone boys.

**Shirley Carroll Smaldone**—Married to Anthony Smaldone. She held the liquor license for Gaetano's.

**Young Eugene Smaldone**—Checkers Smaldone's son. Shunned by the family for his drug use and dealing. Also known as Flipper for his malformed left hand.

**James "Jim" Spinelli**—Early soldier for Joe Roma. He later aligned with the Smaldones.

**Joseph "Scotty" Spinuzzi**—Pueblo's last known Mafia boss.

**Ova Elijah "Smiling Charlie" Stephens**—Gambler and owner of the Blakeland Inn near Denver.

**Joseph "Joe Valley" Valentich**—Friend, driver, and drinking companion of Checkers and Clyde Smaldone.

**Paul "Fat Paulie" Villano**—Smaldone nephew who specialized in bookmaking and loan-sharking with Chauncey Smaldone.

# CONTENTS

Clyde Smaldone's two sons, Chuck, *left*, and Gene. © Kevin Kreck

# FOREWORD

I remember...

Yes, I remember my brother, Gene, next to me, kneeling, his head bowed, his hands bracing his forehead and partially covering his eyes. It was a sad day for us. Our dad was dead, and we were at his funeral. The chapel was filled to capacity, and there were many more mourners outside. All were gathered to pay their last respects to Clyde George Smaldone.

After someone passes, it is a time for reflection and remembering, and my brother and I have shared memories of our father many, many times. It often surprises both of us what sticks in our minds and that many of our memories are so similar.

Gene remembers that when he was a little boy, he never knew what Dad did for a living. Dad would get up early in the morning, usually about 6 AM, have a big breakfast, and leave. He would return home around five o'clock, and the family would have dinner. Gene thought Dad had a job, just like the other kids' fathers. One of the first things Dad did when he came home was to empty his pockets onto the dining room table, creating great rolls of money in several piles: one was gambling money, one was loan money, and the last was his own money. Fifteen years later, when I was a child, Dad repeated this same daily routine. Like Gene, I thought Dad went to work just like my playmates' fathers. After all, he was just "Dad" to us.

All families have skeletons in their closets. For the most part, the skeletons stay concealed behind closet doors. Every family—every one—has both good and bad, but the good is usually the most visible. With the Smaldones, it was quite the opposite: the bad was always out in the open, center stage. And those skeletons were not only out of the closet, they were dressed to the nines and ready to go out to opening night at the opera.

Conversely, behind solid closet doors hung suits of generosity for those less fortunate, overcoats of love for family, and numerous finely tailored outfits of genuine softheartedness, all there but unseen by most of the world.

I hope this book will provide the key to unlocking that door and showing the good side of Clyde Smaldone. He was a person who, at his final tally, had a "Good" column that was far greater than most imagined. Clyde was a man of earthly wisdom who confronted life on his own terms and never glossed over the questionable or illegal. He believed that you are what you are, good and bad, and that you should always face the reality of your existence.

Upon reading Harper Lee's novel *To Kill a Mockingbird*, I realized one of the book's more significant themes was embodied in the character Boo, a ridiculed and isolated man unjustly labeled his entire life as a person without value. But his true good surfaced during a time of great need and danger, displaying a warmhearted, valuable being who had much to offer.

Before reading Lee's great novel, I often felt the world wrongfully judged my father, seeing only a one-dimensional "gangster" when he was so much more that was good and positive. I know that Boo was a person who suffered from debilitating psychological personality traits, but Lee created this unusual character of extremes so that readers would not miss the theme so important in *Mockingbird*. Lee believed, as I do, that no matter the individual—a mom, a dad, a brother, or a next-door neighbor—the true value and quality of a person can never be realized without putting on that person's shoes and walking around the block in them. Only then can someone fairly judge and know that person and the forces that drive him.

I'm confident that this book gives readers the opportunity to put on my dad's shoes and take a stroll. I'm sure you will be surprised, even amazed by what you will discover about Clyde Smaldone. As you read, you might find a tear or two in your eyes, followed by a smile, and, perhaps, even laughter. But most significantly, you will find the true Clyde Smaldone and the real family around him.

Yes, I remember…

—Chuck Smaldone

"Do you know how to keep a secret? Don't tell anyone."

That was a witticism my dad, Clyde Smaldone, used to confront people with frequently. Although people laughed at the answer to his riddle, I think this concept was a strong part of my dad's beliefs. Living up to his own advice of "don't tell anyone," when he was approached about writing a book on his life, he always declined. However, he told me, "You know, maybe after I die it's up to you and your brother about writing a book."

Consequently, several years prior to his death, Dad spent many—sometimes trying—hours with me, tape-recording descriptions of segments of his life with the promise that nothing was to be printed until after his death. It would be a secret.

During our taping sessions, memories often would be triggered about the life and times Dad and I shared. One twinkle of a memory recalled a time when I was a little boy. Dad was reminiscing about the "old" Tejon Bar on Tejon Street between Thirty-seventh and Thirty-eighth avenues, and I flashed on "helping" him clean on weekends. On a Saturday or a Sunday, or sometimes both, I got to tag along when he went to clean the bar before it opened. Dad would tell me that he really needed help to clean properly. Most small boys around six or seven believe they are skilled and helpful in almost everything they do, and I did as well—really. Dad explained that I could keep all the money I found on the floor or in the booths. Knowing Dad, I'm sure much of what I discovered was not lost by the previous day's patrons but carefully placed there by him to ensure that my compensation was a lucrative one.

Then Dad would drive me home and Mom would be sure to inquire if I had been worked too hard. How special those times were, and what a valuable lesson to be learned: always work hard, be dependable, and do a good job. Most importantly, never consider yourself too good for any work. My brother, Chuck, later said that Dad impressed him with that same humble approach to work.

Dad wasn't a man to verbalize his emotions, but his actions conveyed his love for his sons. My father and I shared a life interest: football, which I played throughout my school years, including on a scholarship to the University of Denver. Dad played football on a limited basis in his younger years, and we shared his enthusiasm for the rest of his life. As a proud father, he attended most of my games, but his interest in my athletic career was at its zenith in my college years. I'm sure I had the only father at DU who purchased twenty or more season tickets each year, giving the surplus tickets to family and friends. I think he wanted to guarantee a large number of fans cheering the DU Pioneers on to victory. What better way to tell a son "I care"?

Many years later, gathering information and facts about Dad's life on tape was, in itself, an experience of discovering new things about him, as well as being reminded of incidents long forgotten. Taken together, our conversations form a picture not of a one-dimensional man, "the gangster," but rather of a man of many sides, some bad, but a great number of which show a man who was exceptional in many things. For example, Fred Dickerson, many times Dad's attorney, often exclaimed that if it were possible to have a law partner who didn't have a formal education, Clyde would be the fourth partner in the law firm of Dickerson, Morrissey, and Zarlengo.

All in all, our recording sessions were a conglomeration of loud arguments and quiet acknowledgments of experiences that filled our eyes and hearts with tears and a chuckle or two about humorous circumstances that are gone forever. Many times, for me, our sessions involved listening without reacting.

The hours spread over many months produced a picture of an innately charismatic, intelligent man whose wit and humor combined to form a complex individual. Even though he was in his mid-eighties at the time and his memory and grammar were less than perfect, he was the father I lovingly remembered as the true Clyde Smaldone.

Time had weakened the necessity to "keep a secret." So, when an exhibition on the Italians in Colorado opened at the Colorado History Museum, I realized the time was right to tell Dad's story. This time, when Dick Kreck approached me about doing a book, I said yes, and the tapes that Dad and I made came out of fifteen years' storage. Dick and I discussed a plan of action and asked Chuck to take part in this journey that would end only with the book's completion. You now hold the result of that journey in your hands.

— Gene Smaldone

# ACKNOWLEDGMENTS

First, my thanks to Gene Smaldone, Clyde's son, without whom there would have been no book. It was Gene's generosity and curiosity that led me to unexpected corners of the Smaldones' lives. He gave me access to the family and to Smaldone associates that no one else has ever experienced. His friends Ronnie Bay and the late Gil Borelli were key to nudging him into doing the book. And thanks to Gene, too, for all those fabulous Italian lunches. I came to love sausage and peppers.

Chuck Smaldone, Gene's brother, was also helpful in recalling stories about his father, many of which have never circulated outside the family. His frankness about his personal life was appreciated too.

No book sees the light of day without the watchful eye of a caring and vigilant editor. I was fortunate to have Faith Marcovecchio, with whom I worked on a previous book, *Anton Woode: The Boy Murderer*, to redirect my errant thoughts and sentences. And thanks to designer Jack Lenzo for making this book shine.

Thanks also to those at the Colorado Historical Society, the Western History and Genealogy Department of the Denver Public Library, the Museum of Colorado Prisons, the National Archives, and, in particular, to *The Denver Post*, which allowed me total access to its library, a rich archive of Denver history.

There isn't enough gratitude to thank those who had the time and patience to read the early versions of the manuscript, but thanks go to David Wetzel, who describes himself as a "Miss Grundy" when it comes to adhering to correct English usage; former state historian David Halaas; and historian and many-time author Phil Goodstein, who put it all in perspective.

Finally, my thanks to the many people who knew the Smaldones intimately and shared their memories, some of them for the first time. I know it wasn't always easy to speak up.

Riddled by seven bullets, mob boss Joe Roma lies dead on the floor of his North Denver home in 1933. © Denver Public Library, Western History Collection, Harry M. Rhoads, Rh-295

CHAPTER ONE

# LITTLE CAESAR

*Somebody shot him. It don't bother me one way or another.*

—Clyde Smaldone

The two men on his front porch were familiar to Joe Roma. Otherwise, he never would have opened the door to them. He was careful like that.

The little house at 3504 Vallejo Street in the heart of North Denver seemed a safe haven for Roma and his second wife, Nettie, whom he had married on April 14, 1931. The couple had lived in the isolated bungalow, which provided unobstructed views in all directions, for only a few days. The house directly behind theirs was unoccupied, the lot on the north side was empty, and undeveloped blocks covered the south side of West Thirty-fifth Avenue and the west side of Vallejo Street. The nearest neighboring house, 3455 Vallejo Street, was catercorner to the Romas'. Nobody heard the shots that killed him.

The front and back doors to the modest gray stucco house were always locked, and a bodyguard frequently stayed in Roma's home—but somebody got in. Shortly after noon on Saturday, February 18, 1933, the boss of Denver's gangland, the man known as Little Caesar, was riddled with seven bullets, six of them to the head. When Nettie returned home from visiting her mother on Quivas Street, a few blocks away, she found Joe slumped in his favorite overstuffed chair in the front parlor. She thought he had fainted, but when she tried to lift him out of the chair, she saw that he was covered with blood. "Oh! He's dead!" she screamed to no one in particular. She carefully laid his body on the floor and called the police.[1]

Detectives who kept close tabs on Roma swarmed the house. Suspicion immediately fell on "friends"—or at least someone he knew—because no one else could have gained entry to his home. "No stranger could have got into the house," a distraught Mrs. Roma told officers. "Joe wouldn't let a stranger in. I don't know who did it. I don't know of anyone who was coming to see him, or of anyone expected."[2] He apparently had no hesitation admitting his visitors and must have been at ease with them, because while they talked he rested in his high-backed chair, holding his mandolin, which he loved to play, sometimes accompanied by his wife on the piano. On the music stand at his side sat an instruction book, *Singer's Complete Mandolin Methods*.

Evidence at the scene led police to conclude that his killers sat on either side of him, one on the stool at the upright piano next to his chair and the other in a chair across the small room, catching Roma in a crossfire when they unleashed a fusillade from .45 and .38 caliber weapons. In his death throes, Roma kicked over the music stand. A single bullet pierced the mandolin. The unarmed and unsuspecting Roma—two of his handguns were later found in a dresser drawer—was leaking from so many wounds that police at first theorized he had been shot fourteen times. An autopsy revealed only seven entry wounds, but the bullets, fired at such close range, tore through his small body, spraying blood and brains on his chair and the wall behind him.[3]

Nettie Roma, *left*, is comforted by her mother, Mary Greco, minutes after explaining to police how she found her husband's body. "No stranger could have gotten in." © Colorado Historical Society, *Rocky Mountain News*, February 19, 1933

Though police floated several theories—that a drug dealer killed him (he dabbled briefly in drug distribution) or that a rival gangster marked him for death—the only serious suspect was an eastern hit man, Leo Micciche, who was questioned primarily because he had hosted a dinner honoring Roma a few nights before the murder, the kind of dinner that was often a prelude to death in the mob world. It was all a misunderstanding, said Micciche, a guntoter wanted on a murder charge in Detroit who had moved to Denver three years earlier and went by the name Leo Papito. The spaghetti dinner, for which 165 invitees paid $2.75 apiece, was not a gangland send-off, he swore, but to help pay Mrs. Micciche's recent medical bills, and he knew that Roma's many friends would pitch in. The police subsequently released him.

Joe Roma's funeral was as grand a burial as any ever staged in the Mile High City. The pageantry, marveled the *Rocky Mountain News*, could "rival the splendor attending the burial of gangland kings of Chicago." His body lay in a polished copper casket said to have cost $3,000, guarded by two tall candles at its foot. A glass dome covering the casket bore a simple inscription in Old English script: Joseph P. Roma / July 26, 1895–Feb. 18, 1933. An elaborate floral bouquet adorned by a white sash imprinted with the word *Husband* was draped atop the casket.[4]

The brief funeral took place in the darkened parlor where Roma was gunned down, but the room was now awash with dozens of colorful floral arrangements, including a six-foot-tall Golden Gateway display, topped by a star of yellow roses, that cost $125. The widow told bystanders that she bought the Golden Gateway arrangement because

Roma sent a similar one to the funeral of his friend John Pacello, who had died in January a few days after being shot in the abdomen and arm, injuries, he told police, he had sustained while hunting muskrats.

A crowd of 2,000 onlookers—sprinkled liberally with uniformed and plainclothes cops who kept a sharp eye out for trouble and, with luck, Roma's killers—jammed the streets on both sides of the house. Given the cramped quarters and abundance of floral tributes, only a few close friends attended the 2 PM service. For an hour before it began, however, visitors were allowed to pass by the coffin and gaze at Roma's remains through the transparent dome. Though he was a devout Catholic, Roma, whose first marriage ended in divorce, was buried without the church's blessing, said his widow, because of his sudden death and the absence of last rites. After a brief prayer and comments by the funeral director, pallbearers, including Pueblo mob figures Charley Blanda, Joe "The Ram" Salardino, and Tom "Whiskers" Incerto, among others, accompanied the casket to the hearse at the curb. The three-block-long funeral procession, including two flatbed trucks heaped with floral arrangements, wound slowly through North Denver before heading to Crown Hill Cemetery, where Roma, just thirty-seven years old, was entombed in the Tower of Memories.

Joseph Pasquale Roma was born in Calabria, Italy, on July 26, 1895. At least that's what authorities who threatened to have him deported as an undesirable alien said. Roma

As 2,000 Thronged to Burial Services for 'Little Joe'

More than 2,000 mourners and curious surround Joe Roma's home as pallbearers carry Little Caesar's $3,000 casket to a waiting hearse. Watchful police were in the crowd. © Colorado Historical Society, *Rocky Mountain News,* February 23, 1933

maintained that he was born in San Francisco but that his birth records were lost in the 1906 earthquake.

He came by his nickname, Little Caesar, legitimately because he stood only 5 feet 1⅝ inches and weighed a mere ninety-nine pounds. He possessed a high-pitched—some called it shrill—voice. Under dark eyebrows his dark eyes were soft, in contrast to his prominent nose. Whenever one of his many arrests for liquor violations made the papers, he was invariably referred to as "the little grocer of North Denver." This, too, was legitimate, because Roma operated a grocery store at 3420 Quivas Street and lived for a time in apartments behind the store. Police labeled the grocery as nothing more than a front for his gangland empire and a supply house for bootleggers. Roma saw it differently. When he and brother-in-law Frank Greco were arrested a few weeks prior to the fatal shooting, for operating a still in Gilpin County in the mountains west of the city, he exclaimed, "This is terrible! This incident will ruin my grocery business!" Roma also briefly ran an automobile dealership near downtown.[5]

Police weren't amused by Roma or by his operation. The day after the shooting, a police detective told *The Denver Post*, "He was just a little shrimp but he might as well have been of Herculean stature. Those who first saw him laughed at the idea of his being called a gangster. He looked more like an errand boy for a department store."[6]

Roma's rapid rise to the top of the Denver crime pyramid was made possible by the vacuum created when crusading district attorney Philip Van Cise busted up the Lou Blonger gang in 1922. By bribing corrupt government officials, Blonger and his associates ran gambling and bunco operations unimpeded in the city for almost twenty years—until Van Cise's raids, which netted thirty-three members of the gang, including Blonger, in one night. Blonger died in the state penitentiary in Cañon City only five months after he started serving a ten-year sentence.

Roma moved from Brooklyn, New York, to Denver in about 1915 and made his first appearance on the local police blotter in March 1925 on a federal narcotics charge. Through the years, he was arrested many times, mainly on charges of violating federal anti-liquor laws, but was rarely convicted. Local police once warned him to stop construction on an armored car, one he said he needed to protect himself against a rival gang that had made several attempts to "put him on the spot."

Along the way, two of his rivals, Sam and Pete Carlino, who ran mob activity in the southern Colorado steel town of Pueblo, were murdered, elevating Roma to the top of the gang hierarchy. After his arrival from Brooklyn, Roma worked for the Carlino brothers, but he eventually broke away to run bootlegging and racketeering operations in Denver. The rivalry between the Pueblo and Denver factions, fueled by the enormous profitability of illicit booze, was murderous. Police estimated that between 1919, shortly before federal Prohibition became law, and Roma's death in 1933, more than thirty murders, including four law-enforcement officers, took place in the two cities.

In April 1931, Pete Carlino's Denver house, at 3357 Federal Boulevard, was leveled by a tremendous midnight explosion, one everyone assumed was set off by rival mobsters while Carlino's wife and six children were safely in Pueblo. A police investigation revealed the explosion was

Pete Carlino, *left*, and Joe Roma shake hands after Roma posted a $5,000 bond for Carlino in 1931. Both mobsters were shot dead within two years. © *The Denver Post*

fueled by a potent mix of twenty gallons of gasoline, four gallons of linseed oil, three gallons of turpentine, and two gallons of automotive oil. The man behind the blast, it turned out, was Carlino himself. He and three other men were convicted of arson after police found that the home was destroyed to collect $11,500 in insurance to finance the Carlinos' bootlegging operations.

Less than a month later, on May 8, 1931, Sam Carlino was shot down in the kitchen of his North Denver bungalow. Roma presented himself at the Denver district attorney's office five days after the shooting to proclaim his innocence. He told investigators that he was on his honeymoon in Pueblo and didn't know anything about Carlino's murder. "I am engaged in the automobile business and know nothing about gangs. I have nothing to conceal in either my private or business life and am willing to appear here anytime when you have any questions to ask. I can't imagine how authorities received this misinformation that I am associated with gangsters."[7] In September, Pete Carlino, whose abrasive personality frequently put him at odds with other gang leaders, was found dead near a bridge twenty-two miles southwest of Pueblo, shot three times with a .38. His killers moved his body to a more visible location after it went unnoticed for several days.

In the two years following the Carlino brothers' deaths, Roma's continuing rise to power also elevated the importance of his "friends." Among Roma's confederates were four young toughs: Jim Spinelli, Louis Brindisi, and two streetwise and ambitious brothers, Clyde and Eugene—known as Checkers—Smaldone. By coincidence, or perhaps not, three of the four were in Roma's home only minutes before he was fatally shot. Spinelli, Brindisi, and Checkers freely admitted to visiting the mob boss. They had an alibi. They had arrived, they said, about 10 AM but left just after noon to take in a movie downtown. Roma, they said, was alive when they left, and Clyde Smaldone, they swore, wasn't there at all.[8]

Nevertheless, all four were hauled in by the police and questioned closely. It would not be the last time their names appeared on a police blotter and in the newspapers. Despite several days of interrogation, detectives could not disprove their stories, including the fact that Checkers stopped to borrow fifty cents from Clyde so he and the others could afford to go to the movies on Curtis Street. After the movie, they told police, they went to get some chili, and it wasn't until they saw Clyde that evening that they heard about Roma's killing.

Six decades later, Clyde Smaldone had a different memory of that day, which he revealed in a series of taped interviews made with his son Gene. According to his account, he was there. He said, "[Somebody] shot him in his house. [The police] thought we did it because we left the house about two hours before he got shot. Well, they knew we didn't do it, but somebody shot him. It don't bother me one way or another. [The Pueblo mobs] was always arguing and fighting amongst themselves about the business, and they weren't capable of handling business, to tell you the truth. They was all right making moonshine, but to sell it, they didn't have a diplomatic way of talking to people to get business. Most of them couldn't hardly talk English."

Ultimately, all four were absolved of Roma's murder. In homage to their late boss, the Smaldones contributed two of the most massive floral arrangements at Roma's funeral.

Police, the newspapers, and the citizenry were becoming fed up with a decade of criminal activity. *The Post* thundered in an editorial: "Joe Roma's assassination emphasizes that 'CRIME NEVER PAYS.' The 'big shot' of today in the gang world is the bullet-riddled target of tomorrow. Greed and envy flourish in gangland. Honor among crooks is an illusion. If they had any honor, they wouldn't be crooks."[9] The *News* joined the clamor for something to be done: "A single gangster is a greater peril to a community than all the Socialist and Communist spellbinders."[10]

Denver police immediately reinvigorated a drive to rid the city of mobsters, begun the previous year when they devised a plan to arrest gang members on charges of vagrancy. A vagrant, said law-enforcement officials, "is a man who has no legitimate occupation, no matter how much money he may possess." Raffaele (Ralph) Smaldone, the patriarch of the family, his sons Clyde, Eugene, and Anthony, and their brother-in-law Albert (Bert) Capra all were charged with vagrancy following a police raid on a Smaldone hangout at West Thirty-fifth Avenue and Mariposa Street, which police described as "a perpetual loafing place for bootleggers, racketeers and gangsters." All received forty-day sentences.[11] Despite requests from the Smaldones for extra visiting hours and special meals, county jail wardens vowed there would be no extra privileges. "It's forty days in jail for the Smaldones," said warden James Norton. "There will be no posies or Park Avenue service. They look no different to me than any other prisoners."[12]

After Roma's death, a stack of clippings, all of which mentioned him, was found in his house. It exhibited one thing: Roma had loved the limelight. His murder was a grand exit from a life of crime that was featured often in detailed newspaper accounts.

Despite all the coverage and attention, Little Caesar's murderers were never caught. And though they may not have been involved in the shooting, the Smaldone brothers benefitted most from it. Denver district attorney Earl Wettengel had told reporters in December 1932 that Clyde and Eugene aspired to succeed Roma as leaders of the Denver gangs.[13] In February 1933, it came true in a spray of gunfire. With Roma's death, the brothers were raised to undisputed leaders of the Denver mob.

Raffaele Smaldone, patriarch of the Smaldone clan, arrived in Denver in 1889, made $30 a month working for the railroad, and fathered eleven children. © Smaldone Family Collection

# CHAPTER TWO

# ARRIVALS

*My dad, he worked at the railroad, $30 a month, and then he got*
*to be a foreman, then he got $40 a month. That's when he put a*
*toilet in the house and a bathtub and got rid of the outhouse.*

—Clyde Smaldone

Raffaele Smaldone was born in Potenza, Italy, in 1882 and arrived in the United States with his parents as a two-year-old in 1884. He quickly became Ralph as his parents, like thousands of other immigrants, began the long process of assimilating into the general population. They settled first in Buffalo, New York, but five years later the family, like many before and after them, set out for the wide-open spaces and bright hopes of the uncluttered West.

The argument can be made that the first Italian immigrant to the Americas was Christopher Columbus, a feat Italians continue to celebrate, despite political pressure. In the nineteenth century, the main influx of Italians to the New World was in South America. The tide of Italian immigrants built more slowly in the United States. In 1850, for example, there were fewer than 4,000 Italians, but by 1880, when emigration began to pick up speed, the numbers rose to 44,000, and to 484,027 by 1900.[1] The 1920 US census recorded 1.5 million Italians in the country.

The earliest arrivals were mainly young, unmarried men—prior to World War I the ratio was eighty men to every twenty women—dubbed "birds of passage" by historians because, like Columbus, they didn't stick around. They left their homes in Italy for financial gain and worked hard to send money back, then returned themselves. Far from home in a strange land, the young men congregated in boardinghouses where transplanted Italian women, substituting for the wives and girlfriends many of the men had left behind in Italy, provided them washing, cooking, mending, and, perhaps just as important, entertainment. Driven by economic hardship and discrimination, they worked as shoemakers, waiters, and tailors, and in menial jobs as laborers and janitors, huddling together in wretched conditions in ghettoes in big eastern cities to save money.[2]

Still, conditions were no worse than those they had fled in Italy. Carlo Levi wrote in *Christ Stopped at Eboli*:

> The peasants' houses were all alike, consisting of only one room that served as kitchen, bedroom, and usually as quarters for the barnyard animals as well, unless there happened to be an outhouse. On one side of the room was the stove, sticks brought in every day from the fields served as fuel, and the walls and ceiling were blackened with smoke. The only light was that from the door. The room was almost entirely filled by an enormous bed, much larger than an ordinary double bed; in it slept the whole family, father, mother and children.[3]

In Colorado, the earliest immigrants were mainly northern Italians, better educated than their southern counterparts and generally solid financially, who became the business and political leaders of the community. The first recorded Italians to reach the state were the Garabino brothers, who arrived from St. Louis in 1859 during the height of the illusory gold-rush era—the Pikes Peak Humbug, some called it—which led many "go-backers" to return home, having gotten only the "Bust" half of "Pikes Peak or Bust." They left when they found that there weren't gold nuggets waiting to be plucked off the ground.

The Garabinos were joined shortly by many of their countrymen.[4] Like the Germans, Italians found the saloon business a good way to move into the merchant class and to serve their communities because saloons also were used as social clubs, banks, and protective associations. The Aiellos, Smaldones, and Zarlengos all began their business successes as innkeepers.[5]

Until the late nineteenth century, there had been no great rush of Italians to the West, an unknown place far from their traditional enclaves in the East. Though more immigrants began to trickle into the Colorado Territory in 1872, the 1880 census could find only 880 Italians in the region, although many itinerant laborers probably went uncounted. An economic boom that hit Colorado in the 1880s meant that there were plenty of backbreaking and dangerous jobs—on the railroad and in the mines and smelters, where workers earned $1.25 to $1.75 a day at the same time union miners received $3 a day. Graveyards throughout Colorado and the West attest to the numbers of Italians who labored in these dangerous trades.

Nor were the jobs easy to come by. Labor contractors, known as padrones, signed lucrative contracts with the railroads and mine owners to supply an ongoing labor force. They were often unscrupulous, charging men who were largely peasants outrageous fees and keeping part of their earnings. "Contractors, taking advantage of widespread illiteracy, particularly in southern Italy, sent laborers to the American West under exploitative conditions," Andrew Rolle wrote in *Westward the Immigrants*.[6] Equipped with little money (the average immigrant arrived with $11 in his pocket) and few skills, the first Italians to land in Colorado clustered together in "the Bottoms," a narrow strip of flats along the South Platte River on the western edge of downtown. Clapboard shacks and tents were home. The resourceful Italians found both water and good soil plentiful and began growing a variety of vegetables to sell to supplement their meager incomes. During hard times, their children plucked watercress from the river's edge to be sold downtown, and they sometimes returned with reclaimed cigar butts to sell in the Bottoms.[7]

By the turn of the twentieth century, the North Denver neighborhood, centered at West Thirty-fifth Avenue and Navajo Street, was thriving, and by 1930 there were 10,670 citizens of Italian birth in the city, most living in what came to be called Little Italy. There were drugstores, groceries, bakeries, saloons, social clubs, and restaurants, all Italian owned and operated. There were five Italian-language newspapers. Housewives baked their bread at community ovens. And yet families continued to work hard at having their children become Americanized. Italians also began to gain a foothold in important institutions. August Mattei was the first Italian made a Denver policeman, Prosper Frazzini became a state representative, and

Domenico Lepore and Antonio Campiglia worked in the assessor's office in the powerful administration of Mayor Robert Speer.[8]

But they were not always welcome. The new arrivals faced more than prejudice from nativists, who found the Italians' dark skin, religion, unfamiliar food, and language threatening. Their children had stones thrown at them on public streets. In *Lynching in Colorado 1859–1919*, historian Stephen J. Leonard recounted barroom fights and riots between "Americans" and Italians that ultimately led to one of the most notorious incidents, the public hanging of Daniel Arata by a mob in 1893.

Arata, twenty-eight, was accused of beating and shooting to death a sixty-year-old, down-on-his-luck Civil War veteran named Benjamin Lightfoot who couldn't pay for a second five-cent glass of beer Arata served him at Arata's saloon in the seedy Hotel d'Italia on Wewatta Street. The drunken Arata was taken to the new Arapahoe County jail to await trial.

The next night, a mob estimated to have swelled to 10,000 and egged on by repeated chants of "Lynch the dago!" stormed the jail. A leader of the mob asked the sheriff, "Did we fight to save this country for dagos or for Americans?" The mob dragged Arata from his cell, hanged him from a nearby cottonwood tree, then, for good measure, shot him twenty times and dragged his body to Seventeenth and Curtis streets, where they hanged him again from a telegraph pole.[9]

There were similar immigrant-fueled incidents throughout Colorado, most notably the notorious Ludlow Massacre in southern Colorado in 1914 in which at least twenty people, including two women and eleven children, were killed by Colorado National Guard troops during a strike against Colorado Fuel & Iron by the United Mine Workers of America. Low wages and dangerous working conditions prompted miners, mainly from eastern and southern Europe and Mexico, to go on strike. Mine owners responded by getting the governor to call in guardsmen—really little more than street thugs—who waged war on the workers.

The threat was sometimes internal. "One of the most horrible crimes that ever cast a silhouette athwart the darkened pages of criminal history" occurred in October 1875 in the lower reaches of Denver when a gang of thugs intent on robbery burst into the disheveled shack of Guiseppe Peccorra, a scissors sharpener, who shared the place with three young musicians.[10] The gang of seven Italians and a Mexican, led by Filomeno Gallotti, Michiele Ballotti, and George Valentine, slit the throats of the four men, mutilated their bodies, and tossed them in the cellar. The gruesome murders only confirmed what the general populace already believed: that the Italian neighborhood and its foreign element were to be avoided because both were violent.

Even worse, the citizenry felt so separate from the Italian community that there was no outcry to avenge the four men's deaths. All eight robbers were eventually caught and put on trial, but none was hanged. Gallotti, Ballotti, and Valentine were sent to prison for life, and the others were given lesser sentences.

To an outsider, the Italian neighborhood in the Bottoms appeared homogenous; in fact, regional rivalries from the Old Country were transplanted to the new land. The northern Italians were disdainful of their southern, rural countrymen. It was the southern Italians who poured into the United States in the decade between 1890 and 1900, yet they still made up only 1.5 percent of the immigrants. Germans, Swedes, Jews, Poles, and Serbs also claimed their part of the pot in Colorado.

The Catholic Church and fraternal groups became the backbone of the new Italian "village." At first, Italian worshippers in North Denver attended Catholic Mass at Saint Patrick's Church, 3233 Osage Street, but yearned for an edifice of their own because Saint Patrick's was mainly an Irish congregation. The Irish were happy to see them go elsewhere. The Italians built the first Our Lady of Mount Carmel Church in 1894. When it burned down, they built the present facility at West Thirty-sixth Avenue and Navajo Street, opened in 1904. As it did for many of their neighbors, Mount Carmel played an important role in the lives of the Smaldones. In addition, settlement houses, frequently extensions of religious groups, provided classes in English, sewing, and music and often had gymnasiums, libraries, and day care.

Excluded from membership in "American" clubs and organizations, the Italians turned inward to Italian social clubs. One of the largest such clubs was *Societa Nativi di Potenza Basilicata*, or the Potenza Lodge, founded in 1899 to help immigrants from the Basilicata region of southern Italy find jobs and housing. Unfortunately, lodge members, like their American brethren and their clubs, excluded from membership those not from Potenza and the surrounding area, leading to squabbling among their countrymen and to the formation of other social organizations. By 1922, there were fifteen Italian societies in Denver, including *Unione Fratellanza Italiana*, *Bersaglieri* *Principe di Napoli*, and the Garibaldi Society.[11]

Celebrations also gave Italians a chance to remember their culture. One of the biggest was the feast of Saint Rocco, supported by the Potenza Lodge, which continues to this day every August. Members bid for the right to carry the statue of Saint Rocco through the streets of North Denver.

The grandest celebration of all was Columbus Day, something on which all Italians could agree. Commemoration of the Italian explorer began in 1887, but it wasn't until 1907 that October 12 became an official state holiday; Colorado was the first state to recognize Columbus Day with this observance.

Gaetano and Katrina Smaldone, both of whom were born in Potenza in the 1840s, were among those who arrived in the midst of the late 1880s immigration boom, sailing from Naples for New York City in 1884 with their two small sons, Raffaele and Luigi. After a five-year stop in Buffalo, New York, they landed in Denver in 1889.

In 1901, their son, Raffaele, nineteen years old, married Mamie Figliolino at Mount Carmel Church, a union that lasted until his death in 1938 and produced, in quick succession, eleven children, nine of whom grew to maturity. Corinne was the firstborn, in 1903, followed by Clyde, Eugene (known from childhood as Checkers), Angeline, Anthony,

Mamie Smaldone stands with her six sons, *from left,* Clyde, Anthony, Clarence, Eugene, Andrew, and Ralph, in front of the family bar on Tejon Street in about 1940. © Smaldone Family Collection

Andrew, Ralph, Genevieve, and Clarence (Chauncey), all of whom squeezed into a two-story house at 3427 Osage Street. The parents slept in a bedroom downstairs, and the nine kids slept upstairs, dormitory-style, with the three girls in one small room and the six boys sharing the front bedroom. "We lived up there, and we had an outhouse in the back of the house. We had no bathroom; we'd wash in a tub. My mother would wash four of us at a time about once a week," Clyde recalled.

But things were looking up. Raffaele first landed a job as a laborer with the Denver & Rio Grande Western Railroad, making $30 a month. "Then he got to be a foreman, then he got $40 a month. That's when he put a toilet in the house and a bathtub and got rid of the outhouse." Eventually, the elder Smaldone quit the rigors of toiling on the railroad and took up life as a fruit and vegetable peddler. He pulled together enough money to buy a horse and wagon and began delivering to homes all over town, including the wealthy neighborhoods on Capitol Hill. Clyde recalled those days warmly. "I used to go with him when I was about ten and then I'd go sell newspapers, too. We made pretty good money. I carried stuff in for the ladies and all of that."

The boys contributed in other creative ways. Clyde and Checkers hung around the railroad tracks that traversed the Platte Valley and hurled rocks at the steam-locomotive crews as they passed by. The men would respond by throwing chunks of coal, which the boys carried home to help heat the house.

That Clyde labored in the fruit and vegetable business with his father was not unusual. Italians, used to hard work in the Old Country, expected their sons, especially first sons,

Clyde Smaldone, a handsome, dark-haired young man, attended
North High School but quit in the eleventh grade to help his father
with the family grocery business. © Smaldone Family Collection

to work to help out, perhaps even to the exclusion of education. Young Clyde Smaldone was up to the task. "I went to sell newspapers when I was seven or eight years old. Used to go downtown all by myself, walking over the Twentieth [Street] Bridge. Later, when my brother [Checkers] got to be five and I was nine, I'd take him with me."

The two boys frequently left their familiar surroundings in Little Italy and trudged two miles to downtown to work selling newspapers on street corners. "We had one place we'd sell [*The Post*] at nighttime at Sixteenth and California, and in the morning when we'd get down there early, we'd sell at Fifteenth and Stout, the *News*."

Clyde and Checkers often labored from morning until night peddling papers that cost one or two cents, and were taking home fifteen or twenty cents a day. "We used to get tired; we'd have to walk home. Sometime, we'd have an extra nickel and we'd buy a hot tamale and eat it. We'd take the money home to Mother, and she'd be so tickled to get it. Then the others was born, and we kept selling papers." There was the occasional windfall, too. Clyde and his brother were excited to rush home one evening and tell their mother the good news. "My brother found a five-dollar bill. He didn't know what it was, and I didn't either. So we took it home and give it to my mother. She got scared. She closed the front door and the back door. 'Did you steal that? Where'd you get that?'" Frightened, Clyde confessed. "I said, 'What is it, Mama?' She said, 'That's money!' I said, 'No, a lady gave it to Genie [Checkers].' Which she did, this lady gave him a five-dollar bill."

Raffaele eventually found another avenue for making money: bootlegging. For Italians, wine was an important part of social life, and they were puzzled that government would outlaw such a social lubricant, which was safer to drink than much of the available water. When Colorado voted for Prohibition in 1916, four years ahead of the nation as a whole, Raffaele began selling moonshine to speakeasies in the Bottoms and lower Denver. His conduit: Clyde and Checkers, who went to work as "runners" for their father in their teenage years.

Gleeful friends, *clockwise from lower left*, Clyde Smaldone, Checkers Smaldone, Joe Veccharelli, and an unidentified fourth celebrant mark the end of Prohibition after passage of the Twenty-first Amendment. © Smaldone Family Collection

# CHAPTER THREE

# BOOTLEG

*[Bootleggers], they'd run the bottles from where they'd hide 'em...*
*We'd go get a couple of bottles and sell 'em. They'd sell 'em for $2;*
*we'd sell for $1. Later...we found out where some big ones was,*
*five-gallon kegs, and we stole them too.*

—Clyde Smaldone

The boys saw an opportunity and took it. When he was fourteen years old, Clyde Smaldone and his friend Gerald Nevins exercised their entrepreneurship: they stole booze.

"That was the bootleg days," Clyde remembered. "Gerald says, 'I know where they hide some of their whiskey. We can make money off of that, Clyde.' So we used to watch the bootleggers. They'd run the bottles from where they'd hide 'em into the bars to serve the shots. We'd go get a couple of bottles and sell 'em. They'd sell 'em for $2; we'd sell for $1. Later on, Gerald and I, we found out where some big ones was, five-gallon kegs, and we stole them too. Gerald was two years older than me. We found out where some bootleggers was hiding good whiskey."

There was money to be made, but not as much as they might have made had they been older and much wiser. The pair ransacked garages for liquor in North Denver and around town, not sure what they were taking but sure that booze-thirsty citizens would gladly pay for it. To Smaldone and Nevins, booze was booze. They acquired it where they could. Clyde wasn't good with names when he got older, but he remembered where the booty came from. "I stole from Cody and Jimmy Zito and Goose. We stole quite a few pints from them. Then we stole from the Jews, a lot of five-gallon kegs; that was [Mike] Winchell. He was a big dealer then.

"There was a bonded guy would sell bonded whiskey, an Irishman. We followed him one time, and he had a lot of bonded whiskey in a garage, and me and Gerald, we stole it all. But we didn't have the sense enough to get what we should have got out of it, because we didn't know the price of liquor. We sold many of those bottles for $2, and he was getting $20 for one of them bottles. For the rich people to drink, you know. When they had parties."

It was a booming enterprise, and Clyde, ever the calculating businessman—a trait he would use to his advantage throughout his life—saw the possibilities. "I said, 'Gerald, let's go in partners together.' Gerald said, 'Naw,' so I said, 'I'm going to start bootlegging myself.' I went in with Roxy Stone. Him and I went in partners. I was about nineteen, twenty, right in there. I stayed partners with Roxy for quite awhile and then, [when Checkers] got old enough, we didn't stay with Roxy. I took my brother and we moved our office down on Thirty-fourth and Pecos, and we bought whiskey and sold it, and we made our own. We had some good customers, and we made good money, and we started helping Mother and Dad and bought toys for the kids and clothes for my dad and clothes for my mother and sisters and fixed the house up good. [My brother] Anthony came to work for us too, afterwards. We had problems with the cops, [but] we worked that problem out all right." To Clyde, "working out the problem" meant appeasing local police, either through outright bribery or gifts to family members. Even that wasn't foolproof, Clyde lamented. "There were some of them you couldn't pay."

Practically giving away high-priced liquor in his early days in the bootlegging business, Clyde Smaldone quickly learned the potential financial return from good booze. By the late 1920s, business was good and the money was in bonded products, "the good stuff." By law, bonded whiskey had to be unblended, from one distiller and one distillery, and aged at least four years.

They used hopped-up Fords outfitted with overload springs to disguise the fact that they were hauling heavy cargoes of illicit booze. They were similar to the Fords Clyde used when he first got into the bootlegging trade as a teenager. His favorite was a blue roadster with three spotlights mounted over the windshield. "It was a pretty one. Every time we'd park it anyplace, all the girls would come and look at the car. They wanted to go riding in it, so we took some of them for rides in the car. A lot of people took pictures of it because it was funny with the three spotlights on the windshield."

At first the Smaldones ran liquor between several Midwest cities and Denver. Clyde even enlisted the aid of the Capone mob. "I went up to Chicago and got talking about getting the stuff up in Canada. They said, 'Hell, we get a lot of stuff out of there too. Maybe we can work out something a little better.' I told them how much I paid [$66 a case at the time] and he said, 'Gee, I'm gonna talk to Al [Capone] about that.' I told them where I could load it, where they could bring it across the Mississippi to

Chicago mob boss Al Capone helped the Smaldones get cheaper
bonded liquor out of Canada during the 1920s. Clyde visited
Capone shortly before his death in 1947. © *The Denver Post*

Burlington, Iowa. He says, 'Al says to give it to you for $35 a case. We'll only charge you $2 a case [for gasoline and other expenses].'"

Canada, where there was no Prohibition, was the place to go because our northern neighbors continued to crank out good booze, the stuff that brought $20 a bottle. Clyde recalled, "I used to have to get bonded whiskey from other countries so the rich people would be satisfied to be buying 'bottled in bond,' so I'd go to Canada, drive so we could haul about forty-two cases of bonded liquor from Canada. I used to get Four Aces, Chickencock, and Quaker."

The business was so successful it kept Clyde, Checkers, and others on the road for weeks at a time. "I'd say we'd go about an average between the two places about once a month, because we'd sell that much in a month, two loads. It would be about eighty-four cases. The rich people sure liked that; a lot of nice people wanted it, and they didn't want to feed their friends moonshine."

In the world of bootlegging, rigmarole, or bribes—in Clyde's words, "decorating the mahogany"—were an important part of doing business. He developed relationships with guards on both borders. "If there was four on duty, we'd give them four pints of bourbon and four five-dollar bills; that was big money then. They were nice and they needed it. When I come up through the United States I'd have to give two and two, because the Canadians wouldn't take anything because...other people took care of it.

"Then, later on, I used to go to Ottumwa, Iowa, in the bootleg days, you know, because they made the best moonshine and alcohol in the country. But their alcohol was what I wanted more than anything so I could make other articles of whiskey...alcohol drinks. I'd make gin and rum, 'bathtub rum,' they called it, and we made that with that alcohol. I got in [from Canada] either through Washington, Oregon, and then down through California and over. Sometimes I'd go from Michigan and up into Canada, and I'd get a pretty good price. I got a good price. And there were times when I wanted to get good American bourbon; I'd go to Mexico, but down there, both sides you had to 'take care of.'"

The Mexican operation was much more hazardous. "I went to Tijuana and down [to] fifty miles north, back up in the country, from Mexico City. We'd load the bourbon the same way [as they did in Canada], until one of them American guards on this side called me on the side and said, 'You know, them [liquor] dealers are going to tip [them] off, they're gonna knock off your next load if you come with it because they get 10 percent, some of them stoolies, of what they take.'"

Clyde wasn't easily dissuaded; he figured a way out of the trap. "I sent the first car down—they knew the car—that I was going to load, and I sent another car later. Different drivers, different cars. So they didn't pay no attention to that car, they just paid attention to the car that we used to load. So this other car come, we loaded it, sent it across. Both sides, the officials, they let it through. And the next one we went with our car like it wasn't loaded. They stopped it, searched it. There was nuthin' there because we wasn't hauling nothing, but the others got through. I never went to Mexico anymore."

Clyde Smaldone's career as a bootlegger was not without peril. He and his cohorts were arrested a number of times, nabbed holding several gallons of liquor and for hijacking ninety-six pints of whiskey from a truck in 1927. Checkers, Clyde, Jim Spinelli, and Charley Blanda were charged in 1932 with carrying concealed weapons. Checkers was bagged in one of authorities' periodic attempts to appease the public when police raided his home at 3314 West Thirty-seventh Avenue and discovered an arsenal that included four new .35-caliber rifles, two sawed-off shotguns, and a Browning automatic rifle. He wasn't ruffled. "Maybe I like to go hunting," he told the police. "I don't know anything about this gang stuff."[1]

But the sentence Clyde remembered bitterly years later came in 1933, when federal authorities caught his parents, Raffaele and Mamie Smaldone, peddling booze out of their North Denver home. Overlooking his father's alternative barroom business, Clyde maintained that his parents were ignorant of the Prohibition laws, that they were "framed" by the government, and that the real target was the Smaldone brothers and their associates, including Alonzo Love Jr., Louis Brindisi, George Labriola, Anthony Smaldone, Bert Capra, and Blanda. Clyde and Checkers struck a deal with federal prosecutors, pleading guilty to violating federal liquor laws in exchange for their parents' release.

"There was nothing else we could do," Clyde recalled. "So we did plead guilty. So Judge [J. Foster Symes, pronounced 'Simms'], when he sentenced us, he says, 'It's too bad you're coming in front of me for bootlegging. I wish you come up, you was being tried, because all of you should be dead anyhow. Too bad they didn't shoot youse.' That's what this federal judge says!" Clyde was close to recalling Judge Symes's words, but what he actually said was, "My

THE DEATH PEDDLER: "SOM'THIN' TELLS ME I'M GOIN' TO GIT AN AWFUL JOLT!"

An evil bootlegger flees public scrutiny in Wilbur Steele's page one cartoon from *The Denver Post*, which campaigned vigorously for Prohibition. © Colorado Historical Society, *The Denver Post*, October 8, 1921

only regret in this case is that the owners of the still didn't kill you all off. That would have saved the government the expense of bothering with you."[2] The judge's remarks were in reference to a January gunfight at Florissant, a small town in southern Colorado, in which hijackers, driving a sedan and two trucks, swooped in and attacked a large, eight-hundred-gallon bootlegging operation. The still's owners opened fire on the group, which included Clyde and Checkers Smaldone, Charley Blanda, Louis Brindisi, Dave Buccambuso, John Pacello, and a man known only as Papito (probably Leo Micciche), all of whom were linked to Denver mob boss Joe Roma. Pacello, twenty-three, was killed and Buccambuso wounded.

For their guilty pleas in the Prohibition violation involving their parents, Clyde and Checkers each were sentenced to eighteen months in prison at Leavenworth, Kansas, and fined $1,000 apiece. By the time they completed their sentences and came home, Prohibition was history and the Smaldones were on the lookout for new careers.

"Thirsty ones" line up at the Denver jail after their arrests on
liquor charges in October 1927. Local law enforcement was
mostly ineffectual against bootleggers. © *The Denver Post*

# CHAPTER FOUR

# NOBLE EXPERIMENT

*That was good stuff. People paid [a] good price for it. They*
*wanted it for parties and such as that.*

—Clyde Smaldone

Had it not been for Prohibition, Clyde and his pals might not have embarked on such illegal, and lucrative, careers. Beginning in 1920, Prohibition swept across the land with high ideals of creating a more sober and more productive America. Instead, it spawned a thirteen-year period of lawlessness and violence and, in the end, solved nothing. The Eighteenth Amendment to the US Constitution was approved nationally on January 16, 1919, when Wyoming became the thirty-sixth state to ratify, and it went into effect a year later. The amendment was simple in its wording but far-reaching in its results. It read, in part, "After one year from the ratification of this article the manufacture, sale, or transportation of liquors within, the importation thereof into, or the exportation thereof from the United States and all territory subject to the jurisdiction thereof for beverage purposes is hereby prohibited."

Those forty-three words unleashed more than a decade of criminal violence and blatant defiance by otherwise law-abiding Americans. In big eastern cities such as New York, Chicago, Detroit, and Boston, mobsters were quick to fill the liquor void, producing their own beer and smuggling stronger forms of alcohol from outside the United States. The ban also spawned violent mob bosses, including Al Capone, Dean O'Banion, Bugs Moran, Carlo Gambino, and Lucky Luciano, who not only profited from the illegal liquor trade but, in many cases, ran the political lives of their cities. By the mid-1920s, Capone, the world's most famous mobster, was reaping an estimated $60 million a year, tax free. A half-million Americans were involved one way or another in the business of illicit booze.

Colorado was well ahead of the national rush to Prohibition. In November 1914, Coloradans voted to take themselves dry (with a fifteen-month grace period), thanks to well-organized efforts by the Anti-Saloon League, the Woman's Christian Temperance Union, religious leaders, and other groups. Anti-immigration and antilabor prejudices had added to the mix in 1913 and 1914, when unrest among miners, many of them European immigrants, made the general populace fearful of a liquor-fueled uprising among the lower classes.[1] Dry advocates pointed out that at the time, there were 467 licensed saloons and 550 illicit grog shops in Denver. Saloonkeepers failed to take anti-liquor forces seriously, often mocking their efforts, and by the time they woke up, it was too late.

Colorado and six other states (Iowa, Oregon, Washington, Idaho, Arkansas, and South Carolina) went dry at midnight on December 31, 1915, shutting down the state's 1,500 saloons and 500 hotels, restaurants, and drugstores that sold liquor, and 12 beer breweries. One of the first victims of the ban was the prestigious Denver Athletic Club, which had to dispose of its spectacular wine cellar, among the country's finest. What it didn't pour out it sold to club members at hugely discounted rates. Among the sales were all twelve of the only known bottles of 1884 Schloss Johannisberg cognac.[2]

As first passed into law, Colorado's dry period was peppered with loopholes. One was letting residents purchase alcohol for religious and medicinal purposes. Shortly after the law went into effect, the city issued 16,000 prescription forms for doctors, who could prescribe four-ounce doses of liquor for needy patients with each form. One particularly pious congregation was nabbed by authorities for consuming 400 gallons of "sacramental wine" in a month. Under a later revision, individuals were allowed two pints of wine and twenty-four quarts of beer each month for personal consumption. Denver city auditor Fred Stackhouse noted in 1917 that the city issued 59,339 liquor permits to individuals.

Another loophole allowed beer and spirits to be imported for personal use from wet states. Starting in 1916, an estimated $3,000 to $5,000 of whiskey a month was pouring across the Wyoming-Colorado border. One "importer" was nabbed with 2,000 pints of whiskey disguised as olive oil and salad dressing.

Despite several failed attempts to let Denver go its own way on the issue (including a measure to allow beer but not hard liquor), the city joined the rest of Colorado when the state officially went dry on January 1, 1916. The state legislature tightened the law in November 1918, banning any form of alcohol. Citizens were allowed to keep alcohol in their homes, but since its manufacture and distribution were illegal, it was a moot point—although it made enforcement even more difficult.

The last night of legal alcohol, December 31, 1915, passed quietly in Denver. There were no raucous celebrations, bells or whistles, or scenes of rampant debauchery. Newspaper reporters, many of whom may have visited a saloon or two, were disappointed that John Barleycorn faded away with so little fanfare. "The passing of the old order was quiet and peaceful," reported the *Rocky Mountain News*. "It was truly a wake and the spirit of the new year did not even prevail in the hotels where in former years hundreds have been wont to gather to bid farewell to the old year and welcome in the new."[3]

The evening started like one great party. A thirsty public was so anxious to get "one more" that by 9:30 PM on the last day saloons were operating legally, some ran out of alcohol and were forced to pour customers lemonade dyed red to look like wine.[4] Photographers dashed from bar to club to hotel to capture on film the last moments of legal drinking, though it ended early. Even hotels and cafés, where undercover cops were on the prowl for violators, cleaned off their tables by 11:30 and ushered customers out the door.

The curious gathered in front of Henry Weinberger's bar on Curtis Street to get a look at his window display of bottles, jugs, glasses, and funnels, all draped in black crepe. A rusted beer bucket carried a sign: "I was full once. But I can rush the can no longer—all I can do is growl," a reference to "rushing the growler," or getting a bucket of beer to go.

At midnight, small groups of revelers roamed downtown, especially on Curtis Street, where those who had chosen to attend a movie instead of having a last drink briefly honked their horns and blew whistles while vendors worked the crowds, peddling miniature water wagons, a symbol of the dry era. Fifteen minutes later, though, all had gone home and the streets were quiet.

The "honor" of being the first drunk arrested on January 1, 1916, belonged to either John Hanson, forty-nine, a laborer (he was *The Post*'s nominee), or Charles Robbins, thirty-eight, a farmer from Longmont (chosen by the *News*). Hanson drew a round of applause from other prisoners when he was led into jail. Three young men, taking advantage of an exception in the law that prohibited drinking in public places but not on public sidewalks, sat on the curb at Sixteenth and California streets in the heart of downtown and shared a large stein of beer.

In the week that followed, there were a few arrests for drunkenness, but anti-liquor forces were hard at work. The Capitol Brewing Company of Denver was cited for sending ninety-six gallons of beer to a customer in Ault, in the northern part of the state. The owner of the Alamo Hotel was hauled in for keeping sixteen quarts of beer in his hotel's refrigerator. He claimed the beer was for his personal use, allowable under the law as it stood. Police were sympathetic and agreed to let him go if he could prove the hotel lobby was the reception room of his home.[5]

Emboldened, leaders of the Anti-Saloon League tried, unsuccessfully, to force newsstand operators to remove liquor advertisements from magazines and newspapers. References on the windows of former watering holes to the availability of any form of alcohol were painted over. The oddest side effect was the sudden homelessness of hundreds of cats, kept as barroom pets that lived off scraps from free lunches and whose job it was to keep down the rat population. The Dumb Friends League stepped in to provide homes for the pets, even for a wayward bar dog named Madame Butterfly who demanded a beer every morning to start her day.

The law turned saloons into lunch counters or soft-drink parlors and introduced women into the hallowed halls of barrooms, where no self-respecting woman would have been seen before Prohibition. "Dainty, high-heeled feet rested on the familiar brass rail, accustomed in the past to nothing but a trousered tread," said the *News* in wonderment.[6] When low-alcohol beer became available again early in 1933, vigilant reporter L. A. Chapin predicted, "Women will not be heavy beer drinkers. Too much beer will make them fat, and no woman with a beautiful figure or one approaching beauty is desirous of losing it." Women didn't seem intimidated, because he also reported that women freely mingled with men and "lifted the foaming beverage for all to see and downed it with gusto."[7]

Thanks to Clyde Smaldone and dozens of others like him, the state never went totally dry during Prohibition. While others were making and selling homemade booze, Smaldone and his partners were crossing both borders to smuggle bonded whiskey, "real booze." "I sold a lot of that. That was good stuff. People paid [a] good price for it. They wanted it for parties and such as that. So we had everything fixed that we wanted to do and we did all right."

Thousands of average citizens who couldn't afford bonded liquor, from cab drivers to mechanics, were making concoctions at home. There were few enforcement agents to cover 324,000 square miles of the state. They had

Driven from the beer business by Prohibition, breweries advertised barley-malt syrup, with which citizens could make beer. © Colorado Historical Society, *The Denver Post*, May 8, 1931

a particularly difficult time in Denver and Pueblo, where large populations of Italians, who viewed wine as a part of everyday living, never embraced the ban and imported grapes from California to continue making wine.

Locally produced moonshine—known variously as Sugar Moon, so named because it was cooked up from Colorado's plentiful supply of sugar beets, and expensive, cask-conditioned Leadville Moon, made, it was rumored, using black powder and old miners' overalls—was readily available, literally on many street corners. Newsboys for the *News* and *The Denver Times* (owned by the same management) offered customers their illicit products so openly that their pro-dry rival, *The Post*, was moved to complain in a headline: "A Bottle of Booze with Every News."[8]

For its part, the *News* pointed out that Prohibition didn't accomplish what its backers hoped: to reduce public drunkenness. *The Post* confirmed this, citing statistics from city officials, reported in January 1918: "One thousand more arrests in 1917 than in 1916. Eleven thousand jailed. Two thousand and six drunks—a larger proportion than in 1916." These statistics were a made-to-order argument for use by the anti-Prohibitionists: "'Ha! Ha!' shout the champions of booze and beer. 'Does Prohibition prohibit? It does NOT!'"[9]

Everybody who drank claimed a reason, other than enjoying it, for doing so. Parents argued that they were making bootleg at home to ensure the quality of the products their children were consuming because bad liquor could sometimes be poisonous. This wasn't a mere bogeyman used to scare youthful imbibers. There was "the good stuff" and there was everything else, moonshine that ranged from

State Prohibition agents stand amid eighty-nine confiscated moonshine stills, valued at $10,000 by law enforcement, in December 1920. The copper kettles were sold for scrap.
© *The Denver Post*

passable to deplorable and could be "a fluid of dubious origins which caused blindness and other infirmities."[10]

Moonshine produced in unsanitary stills under unsanitary conditions and the addition of alcoholic "kick" using unsavory ingredients, including embalming fluid, rubbing alcohol, or paint thinner, could, in fact, cause blindness. Making moonshine, also known as "corn liquor" or "white lightning," is simple, done easily in a few days by boiling and distilling a soup of corn, yeast, sugar, and water. But if distillation and filtration are done improperly, it can contain highly toxic methanol or traces of lead from the still. Symptoms include abdominal pain, anemia, renal failure, hypertension, blindness, and death.

Moonshine's physical dangers aside, voters had a love/hate relationship with Prohibition. In 1912, for example, Prohibition was voted down in Colorado, 75,733 to 115,879, but the 1914 ban passed 129,589 to 118,017. How much the public's attitude had changed was made clear in a 1926 poll of *Post* readers. "The resulting figures are 'wet—very wet!'" the paper declared in a page-one article. "The Rocky Mountain region—backbone of the Prohibition movement and, for years, rated the most arid section, alcoholically speaking, in the nation—has gone wet, according to the sentiment expressed in *The Post*'s referendum." In the newspaper's informal poll of its readers, Coloradans outside of Denver voted 29,614 to 10,762 to end Prohibition. In Denver, the vote was an even more lopsided 39,431 to 8,762. The vote was equally tilted in favor of a separate vote on allowing beer and wine.[11] Six years later, the state's voters went for repeal of the Eighteenth Amendment by more than 50,000 votes.

Humorist Franklin P. Adams summed up America's relationship with Prohibition in a 1931 poem:

> Prohibition is an awful flop.
> We like it.
> It can't stop what it's meant to stop.
> We like it.
> It's left a trail of graft and slime,
> It don't prohibit worth a dime,
> It's filled our land with vice and crime.
> Nevertheless, we're for it.

Whether you were for it or against it, illegal alcohol and its manufacture often were laid at the feet of foreigners such as the Germans and Irish, who, before Prohibition, were the largest owners and operators of saloons in Denver. E. H. McClenahan, federal Prohibition director for the Colorado district, declared, "Ninety percent of the illicit distillers and purveyors of murderous whiskey in Denver and the rest of this country are unnaturalized foreigners. Every person convicted of breaking the national Prohibition law the second time…ought to be deported as an undesirable alien. They ought to be shown the door."[12]

Despite such strong words, enforcement of the law by federal agents, few in number and ill paid, was spotty at best, and bribes were frequent. There were numerous arrests, but the overcrowded courts were lenient, offering "bargain days," when defendants were allowed to plead guilty in exchange for minimal sentences to clear the dockets. Even early on during Prohibition, Denver district attorney John Rush was less than enthusiastic about enforcing such measures. He would, he said in 1916, prosecute bootleggers and other law violators, but he wouldn't go out of his way to run them down. "This is not a detective agency, and we cannot do the work of the police."[13]

By the mid-1920s, public attitudes favoring Prohibition began to change. There was an increasing realization that Prohibition was costing the country jobs and tax revenues. In a 1925 editorial, *The Post*, which only five years earlier had been gung-ho for the ban, now called for a national referendum on the issue:

> The longer Prohibition goes, the more apparent it becomes that no law ever passed in this country has been so flouted and treated with contempt and contumely. There has been too much hypocrisy about the whole thing. Men, who thru political expediency, supported the dry amendment and the Volstead law have since then done everything they could to defeat the success of Prohibition. That is to say nothing of the tens of thousands of citizens who have been living in a state of open rebellion, and avow their purpose to continue. We ought to get honest about booze again.[14]

By early 1932, it was becoming clear to the public and to bootleggers that Prohibition was on its way out. The dry spell ended with 3.2 beer, a tentative preamble to the coming of total repeal. At 12:01 AM on Friday, April 7, 1933, the first cases rolled out of the Coors brewery in Golden, Colorado, marking the end of thirteen years of "drought" for American beer drinkers. Full repeal loosed a tidal wave

Happy, and thirsty, crowds jammed Denver taverns for 3.2 beer, legalized in April 1933, eight months ahead of national repeal.
© Colorado Historical Society, *The Denver Post,* April 7, 1933

of consumption of full-strength beer in December 1933. It was as though a booze dam had burst. In the week after alcohol became available again, *Post* reporter Bruce A. Gustin told readers, "Drunken men and women, shrieking at the tops of their voices, shattered the Sabbath quiet and made disgusting spectacles of themselves in the big hotels and 'beer joints' which masquerade as restaurants. Laws and regulations were disregarded with brazenness characteristic of the drunken days which shocked the nation into trying Prohibition."[15]

Drinking establishments no longer could be called saloons, a word with negative connotations and a reminder of the rowdy watering holes that infested the city before Prohibition. Instead, they would be called taverns, bars, cafés, or nightclubs. Barrooms put stools at the bar because patrons were required to be seated more decorously at "tables" to drink. In the men-only days, they just stood.

As Prohibition wound down with the return of legally licensed beer parlors, establishments known as "shot joints," perhaps as many as 500, according to police, openly sold hard liquor without licenses, creating unfair competition and costing the city tax dollars.

A fed-up manager of safety, William Guthner, declared in October 1935, "The liquor laws are to be enforced in Denver. The day of the rubber sandwich with drinks has passed." Those unfamiliar with the term may have scratched their heads, but clever tavern owners did not. Guthner ordered that bars had to "offer food of the patron's own choosing"[16] with alcohol by the drink. A sandwich, said the new ordinance, was to cost no more than five cents—to avoid sales tax—and was to be served with the customer's first drink.

Bar owners quickly figured a way around that requirement by preparing one sandwich that made numerous trips between the kitchen and patrons. It became known as a "rubber sandwich." One restaurateur lost his license for repeatedly serving a sandwich that was "at least a week old." Another put down a crust of bread and some crumbs in front of a drinker, who could tell anyone—especially city agents—that he'd already eaten his sandwich.[17]

Colorado's alcohol ban didn't end entirely until repeal took effect in December 1933, after approval of the Twenty-first Amendment, the only provision to wipe out a previous constitutional amendment. As a last gasp to keep alcohol illegal in the state, *The Post* urged its readers to reject Amendment Seven, which would repeal Prohibition in Colorado. "If this amendment is adopted, no drunken sot can be arrested for being intoxicated and no man arrested for trying to drive an automobile while he is drunk. EVERY VESTIGE OF LEGAL PROTECTION WHICH THE PEOPLE HAVE AGAINST BOOZE AND ALL ITS EVILS WILL BE TAKEN AWAY."[18] Despite the overheated rhetoric and ample use of capital letters, the Denver electorate ignored the newspaper and voted two-to-one to end what was called "the noble experiment."

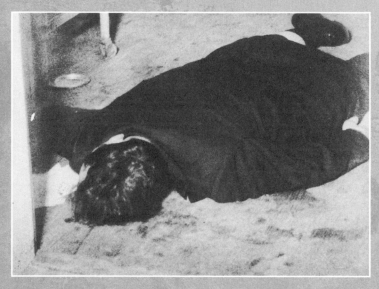

More than thirty gang murders took place in Colorado between 1919 and 1933. Among the victims was Sam Carlino, sprawled on his kitchen floor after being shot. © *The Denver Post*

# CHAPTER FIVE

# MURDER, INC.

*They was always arguing and fighting amongst themselves
about the business.*

—Clyde Smaldone

Nobody took greater advantage of the public's thirst and the federal government's inability or unwillingness to police Prohibition than the racketeers who quickly figured out that there were big bucks to be made from illicit booze. Looming profits led to greed, which led to violence. The period from 1919 to 1933 was the most violent in modern Colorado history, a bloodbath that raged as mobs in the northern and southern halves of the state fought over the lucrative market.

Denver in the 1920s was a city in turmoil. The population soared past 260,000. Well ahead of the coming national depression, Colorado's mining and agricultural industries were in decline, creating a sense of unease among residents. Dewey Bailey, elected mayor in 1919, took a laissez-faire attitude toward vice, just like mayor Robert Speer, who was driven from office in 1912 because of it. Bailey looked away from the excess of saloons and houses of prostitution. Phil Goodstein notes in *In the Shadow of the Klan*, a history of 1920s Denver: "Despite the official outlawing of prostitution, 'rooming houses' lined downtown streets where a man could easily buy the companionship of a woman. Not only did an illicit liquor trade exist, but it was extremely violent, complete with gang warfare, bombings, and shoot-outs."[1] A grand jury investigation into police corruption concluded that "bootleggers, prostitutes, and gamblers have been operating more or less openly and apparently with the knowledge of the police department."[2]

The combination of economic uncertainty and the city administration's reluctance to take a stand against vice was a yawning opening for the Ku Klux Klan, which arrived in Denver in 1921 and promised to preserve and defend the American system. The populace, especially politicians and the city's behind-the-scenes power brokers, welcomed the Klan eagerly because it promised simple answers to complex problems.[3]

The Klan was at the height of its powers in Colorado politics between 1923 and 1926. With the hooded empire's help, Benjamin Stapleton beat Bailey in the 1923 Denver mayoral election; Clarence Morley, a political hack and former district court judge, became governor; and Rice Means was elected a US senator in 1924. Dozens of other Kluxers held jobs in Stapleton's administration.

Smaldone heard about the Klan's antipathy toward anyone who wasn't a God-fearing white American but took it in stride. "[Clarence] Morley was a governor, a good friend of mine. He was head of the Ku Klux Klan, but he wasn't the big head, because Dr. [John Galen] Locke was the big head. The power [Locke] had, he didn't know what to do with it. He could have run for president at that time. In Colorado, every big job was Ku Klux Klan. Our chief of police [William Candlish] was a Kluxer. Stapleton was a Kluxer."

Clyde Smaldone saw an opportunity: to use the Klan's influence, despite its anti-Catholic, anti-immigrant (including Italians), and antiblack proclivities, in part because the Klan's law-and-order pose never hampered the bootleg business. "My dad was in partners with guys [in a speakeasy] and, through me, the Ku Klux Klan used to go down to this bootleg place and drink there." African American policemen who patrolled the rail yards were concerned about the presence of KKK members near where his father's speakeasy was located. Clyde knew enough people in power that he could "fix" things. One officer approached Clyde for help. "They didn't want to walk the beat so they talked to me, and he says, 'Can you do anything?' I says, 'Sure.' I talked to Governor Morley. He says, 'I'll take care of that. Don't worry. Can you talk to the colored guys?' I said, 'Sure,' and I did. I said, 'You're not going to be scared anymore. You come down here, do your work, walk on your beat, whatever you're supposed to. Any problem comes up, you talk to me.' Hell, they was glad to work down there after that."

The Klan and the Smaldones stayed within their own spheres. "They had the power, and they never bothered us either when they were in power. Whatever we wanted to do, they never bothered us because they knew we was feeding all the people who were sick and all that, and they believed in that."

Stapleton was an adept politician. He was mayor through six terms, from 1923 until 1947, and survived a recall attempt, thanks to Klan support, but he oversaw a gang-ridden period; more than thirty violent deaths and unsolved disappearances were tied to the illegal liquor trade in Denver and Colorado in the fourteen years beginning in 1919. They are too numerous to recount individually, but there are several that deserve closer examination.

The first took place on August 29, 1919, when Detective George Klein, head of the Denver Police Department's anti-bootleg squad, was ambushed by three blasts from a shotgun just outside his home in a West Colfax neighborhood. Klein, thirty-four, had been in the news two months earlier for fatally shooting Jerry Corbetta, a young veteran just back from World War I, during a raid on a North Denver soft-drink parlor suspected of serving as a front for a bootlegging operation. Klein testified at a hearing that as he entered the shop, Corbetta ran out the back door. Klein gave chase and fired a warning shot, but Corbetta kept running. As the men raced up an alley, Klein said, he fell and his revolver discharged, striking Corbetta in the back. Klein called the shooting accidental and was exonerated by a coroner's jury. A crowd of 4,000 irate residents of North Denver, mostly Italians, descended on city hall after the young vet's death, demanding that Klein be discharged from the police department. He wasn't. But he was reassigned and never carried a gun again, not even on the night he died.

Klein was gunned down as he exited his car near his home at 1438 Newton Street at about 1 AM on August 29 by an assassin lying in a weed-covered empty lot next door. Heavy buckshot tore into Klein's body, the fatal shot passing through his lungs and severing his spinal cord. As he lay dying on the ground next to his car, his wife rushed from her bed to his side. He gasped, "They got me at last, dearie! Call the boys at the station, and say 'Goodbye' to the kiddies for me."[4]

Investigators were unsure whether Klein's killing was booze related or an outgrowth of his killing of Corbetta. In any case, editors of *The Post* had made up their minds.

Expressing their outrage, the paper intoned in a fiery page-one, two-column editorial headlined "COWARD,"

> In all the putrid category of crime, there is nothing lower, nothing more dastardly than the man—animal would be the better word—who, slinking in the shadows, his own craven body protected by concealment, kills a fellow human being from ambush. But no matter who killed George Klein, that man was a coward.[5]

If Klein's murder demonstrated that even law enforcement wasn't exempt from being targeted, the cold-blooded assassination of patrolman Richie Rose three years later drove home the point. Rose, a thirty-year-old patrolman, joined the department in 1921 and became an ardent opponent of bootleggers. On the morning of October 21, 1922, he was walking his beat in North Denver when he stopped for a cup of coffee at his house at 3718 Kalamath Street. As he walked to the police call box at West Thirty-eighth Avenue and Lipan Street, a fusillade of shots erupted from a Ford touring car parked nearby. Twenty-one shots, some from point-blank range, poured into Rose. His killers were never found.

In response to Rose's death, police chief Rugg Williams ordered closed all North Denver pool halls, soft-drink parlors, and cigar stores police suspected were fronts for bootleggers. Like many other murders of the period, the death of Rose, who was Italian, had familial connections. Mob strong arm Joe Piscipo was arrested in the murder of Pueblo gangster Vicenzo Urso, Rose's brother-in-law, in 1922, then was himself killed on July 3, 1924. Joseph

Spinuzzi, another Pueblo guntoter and a suspect in the murders of both Piscipo and Urso, was shot down in July 1924, three weeks after Urso.

Many of the murders were related to the rivalry of gangs in Pueblo and Denver, which operated independently as the 1920s dawned. In Pueblo, bootlegging and protection rackets were run by two groups: the Danna brothers, John, Tony, Pete, and Sam, working out of the small southern Colorado town of Trinidad, and the Carlino brothers, Sam and Pete, of Pueblo. In Denver, there were a number of independent operators, but the "big boss" was Joe Roma. The Carlinos and the Dannas were constantly at war, with bodies piling up on both sides. "They was always arguing and fighting amongst themselves about the business," Clyde Smaldone said years later in dismissing the warring gangs.

Things heated up in Pueblo in 1925 when John Danna was shotgunned to death by an unknown assailant lying in wait in a ditch on the Danna farm outside Pueblo. More shootings followed. A particularly gory episode took place on May 14, 1926, on the streets of Pueblo, where brothers Tony and Pete Danna stood in front of the Monte Carlo Pool Hall. Suddenly, a large Hudson roared past and the muzzles of three sawed-off shotguns poked through its closed side curtains. The car's assassins blazed away, and, police estimated, each of the Dannas was hit by thirty to forty pieces of buckshot, literally shredding their bodies. Both were taken to a hospital, where Tony died without revealing anything to police, but Pete said before he died that he recognized four men in the car: Pete and Sam Carlino and John Mulay Jr. and Carlo Mulay—the two sets of brothers battling the Dannas for control of the rackets in

Pueblo. The fourth Danna brother, Sam, was shot in 1928 but lived, only to be taken for a ride, shotgunned, and discovered dead in a Pueblo alley four years later. No one was ever charged in any of the murders, but the Dannas' deaths later were linked directly to several other killings.

With their main rivals out of the way, and now firmly in charge in southern Colorado, the Carlinos decided to expand their market by going into business with Joe Roma in Denver. The Carlino-Roma partnership was short-lived. Only four months apart early in 1931, both Sam and Pete met the same fate as the Dannas.

The carnage was all about territory and profits. Like the rest of the United States, bootleg bosses were feeling the pinch of the Depression, which threw millions out of work and dried up the country's cash flow. Colorado survived the early years of the Depression relatively unscathed, but by 1931 things were getting grim, money was becoming scarcer, and more and more civilian entrepreneurs were supplementing their incomes with moonshine. "Price-cutting is the crux of the situation" was one police official's assessment. "Every liquor outfit is trying to cut the other gang's throat." In 1925, moonshine cost $2 or $3 a pint and the good stuff—"What there is of it," said one supplier—was $6 to $10 a pint. By 1931, the price of a pint of moonshine tumbled to as little as 35 cents. It seemed everyone was in the business. In addition, local and federal police were cracking down on bootleggers and many, including Roma, were given prison sentences.

Heavily armed hijackers indiscriminately grabbed the beer and liquor outputs of their rivals. Pete Carlino, bent on crashing the lucrative liquor trade in Denver, was accused

Brothers Sam, *left*, and Pete Carlino ran Colorado mob activities out of Pueblo until both met untimely deaths, Sam in May and Pete in September 1931. © *The Denver Post*

of hijacking forty kegs of liquor and kidnapping the men guarding it. The booze and the boys were returned, but Carlino sent a chilling warning: "You got your booze back and you were darned lucky to get your men back. But what happened is just a sample of what may happen if you don't play with me."[6]

Faced with political pressure, Denver police periodically undertook clean-up drives, arresting known gangsters as "vagrants." ("If a man's habitual associates are police characters, that fact justifies a charge of vagrancy," said one magistrate.) They raided speakeasies and promised to "get tough" with the criminal element. It rarely worked. Once the heat was off, the bootleggers blithely resumed their trade. *The Post*, virulently opposed to the do-nothing administration of Mayor Stapleton, campaigned in its columns to rout him from office. The paper portrayed the city administration, particularly Chief of Police Robert F. Reed, whom it repeatedly branded "Diamond Dick" for his love of flashy jewelry, as paralyzed with fear and in denial of gangsters running amok. It printed a mocking takeoff on a popular novelty tune of the day, "There Ain't No Flies on Auntie," entitled "There Ain't No Crime in Denver":

> No racketeers in Denver
> Where, Denver? Yes, Denver.
> No rackets here in Denver.
> That we've heard, and here's why:
> Of rackets we have no fear—
> We just stuff cotton in our ears,
> And silence 'em in Denver.
> Chief Diamond Dick and I.[7]

There were several more choruses, each no more musical but just as damning.

In January 1931, Captain Albert T. Clark, one of the city's most ardent crime fighters, who promised the police would give no quarter to mobsters, said, "It's a fight to the finish. We will permit no liquor markets here, for once they gain a foothold, it is virtually impossible to stamp them out."[8] Clark sternly warned Pete Carlino and his partners, who included Clyde Smaldone's boyhood pal Gerald Nevins, "Denver police are ready for you guntoters. You start anything and police will finish you with machine guns."[9] One month later, Clark and his lieutenants arrested bootleggers after a sweep by six agents through North Denver pool halls and so-called soft-drink parlors, twenty-one of which were summarily closed. Clark told his men, "Close those places and see that they stay closed. If members of these liquor gangs do not have a specific place to congregate, there will be less trouble."[10] Three of Carlino's bodyguards were among those swept up.

But local efforts weren't enough. Denver police went to federal officials in March 1931 to get help in stemming the lawlessness. Pushed by civic groups and local newspapers, the city administration "openly admitted, for the first time, that a gang situation actually exists here."[11] Federal help came in the person of US attorney Ralph Carr, appointed in 1929, who would later serve as Colorado governor and an important figure in Clyde Smaldone's criminal career. Unfortunately, the federal-local effort came to naught when the two sides accused each other of botching their side-by-side investigations.

The whole killing spree might have been stopped in January, when Pueblo and Denver factions held a "summit

And It Had to Happen Just Before Election, Too!

Denver mayor Ben Stapleton and police chief Robert "Diamond Dick" Reed were lampooned for failing to curb gang violence. © Colorado Historical Society, *The Denver Post*, May 9, 1931

meeting" at La Palmarte restaurant in suburban Denver. More than two dozen men linked to crime syndicates from all parts of Colorado sat down to a chicken dinner to organize the state's illicit liquor trade, including setting territories and minimum prices. An untimely police raid put an end to the meeting, which ironically turned out to be totally dry. Thirty police officers armed with submachine guns burst in but found only a banquet in progress, without booze "on the table, under the table or in the kitchen." It's likely someone tipped the principals to the impending raid.

Police hauled in twenty-nine attendees the night of the raid—and, for good measure, another four in subsequent days—although the charges were vague beyond "investigation," an opportunity to question them about the local liquor industry. Police took credit for nipping in the bud a plan for organizing local bootleggers. "[A] major part of the plan of [the] organization was to establish a price of $4 a gallon as the manufacturers' price," Captain Clark told a reporter. "From this was to be deducted twenty-five cents to be placed in...a sort of protective fund to be used for such members when arrested, for bonds, and for attorneys' fees." The cartel, he said, also planned to maintain a retail price of $10 a gallon and $2 a pint.[12]

With the interruption of the summit, the liquor trade and the violence that trailed in its wake went on its way, without boundaries. Now, not only did bootleggers have to keep an eye out for the law, they had to be alert to hijackers and rival mobs moving in on their markets. In 1931 and 1932, there were twelve shootings or disappearances, including federal anti-bootleg agent Dale Kearney, gunned down on the main street of Aguilar, Colorado, and federal agent L. L. Baldesareli, wounded in front of a downtown Denver hotel. It was Baldesareli, working undercover in the mob, who had scoffed at local newspapers' fixation that the spree of murders was connected to the Black Hand, a clandestine Sicilian group that wrote extortion death threats to other Italians: "Gangsters don't write letters. They use bullets," said Baldesareli before being wounded.[13]

A mere ten months after diminutive mob boss Joe Roma was gunned down in his living room, Prohibition ended, and so did the tit-for-tat killings. The last of the old-style gangsters to die by gunfire was twenty-three-year-old Augie Marino, whose real name was August Caputo. On May 5, 1933, he was "taken for a ride," just as in popular gangster-movie plots, and his body dumped in a ditch in Adams County, five and a half miles north of Denver city limits. He had been shot twice in the head and once in the chest with a .45. Marino, closely connected to both Checkers and Clyde Smaldone when they all worked for Roma, was still on crutches after being shot the previous December in an attempt to hijack whiskey. Police speculated that Marino, who bragged to his pals that he feared "nothing or nobody," was killed because he had aspired to replace Roma.

In the days after Marino's death, close on the heels of Little Caesar's and the Carlino brothers' murders, the era of the bootlegging, guntoting gangster and the liquor-drenched speakeasies, often viewed as a romantic revolt against the establishment, was coming to a close. With the legalization of alcohol, the Smaldone clan was out of the liquor business. Clyde Smaldone and his brother Checkers didn't have far to look to find another illegal trade to ply, however. Soon a very lucrative business would take liquor's place: gambling.

# Gang Murders

During the Prohibition-era mob wars that raged in Colorado between 1919 and 1933, an estimated thirty or more men were gunned down. Killings between the Pueblo and Denver mobs became a tit-for-tat situation, but most of the murders went unsolved. Among the victims were mobsters, law-enforcement officers, and relatives of mob members. Cities listed are where they were killed.

**August 29, 1919**—Detective George Klein, Denver

**May 6, 1922**—Tony Viola, Pueblo

**October 31, 1922**—Policeman Richie Rose, Denver

**February 27, 1923**—John Mulay Sr., Pueblo

**June 19, 1923**—Vicenzo Urso, Pueblo

**September 10, 1923**—Dominick Ingo and Carlo Carlino, Pueblo

**July 3, 1924**—Joe Piscipo, Pueblo

**July 21, 1924**—Joseph Spinuzzi, Pueblo

**April 28, 1925**—Frank Lucia, Pueblo

**July 16, 1925**—John Danna, Pueblo

**April 13, 1926**—Frank Bacino, Denver

**May 14, 1926**—Tony and Pete Danna, Pueblo

**July 1, 1928**—F. H. Holliman, Denver

**October 26, 1928**—H. Nobile, Pueblo

**November 5, 1928**—Paul Dean, Denver

**April 28, 1929**—Peter Percel, Fort Collins

**May 10, 1929**—Joe Clark, Denver

April 8, 1930—Hilario Clemmoure, Denver

April 13, 1930—William Gallagher, Pueblo

April 30, 1930—Andrew Lombardi, Colorado Springs

May 6, 1930—Sam Danna, Pueblo

July 6, 1930—Federal agent Dale F. Kearney, Aguilar; Federal agent Ray Sutton, disappeared (date uncertain)

February 17, 1931—Ignacio Vaccaro, disappeared (presumed dead)

April 3, 1931—Carlo Maurello, Pueblo

May 8, 1931—Sam Carlino, Denver

May 10, 1931—Joe Farrell, missing, presumed dead in California

September 14, 1931—Pete Carlino, found in Pueblo

January 16, 1932—Murrell C. Rothfus, Denver

March 17, 1932—Vincent Mortellaro, Denver

June 17, 1932—Maurice Cohen, Denver

June 25, 1932—Bert Adams, Denver

January 24, 1933—John Pacello, Pueblo (shot on this date, died January 28)

February 18, 1933—Joe Roma, Denver

May 5, 1933—Augie Marino (August Caputo), Denver

Born in Denver in 1906, Clyde Smaldone detested the nickname Flip-Flop, hung on him by a newspaperman. His career in rackets spanned the 1920s to the 1960s. © *The Denver Post*

# CHAPTER SIX

# CLYDE

*We fed the people and done good to the people...I was glad to do it. It made me feel good. I slept good nights then, too. Even when I went to prison I used to think about that.*

—Clyde Smaldone

The first thing to know about Clyde George Smaldone is that he was never known as Flip-Flop. Not to his family. Not to his friends. And definitely not to his face.

Flip-Flop was the colorful nickname hung on him in the early 1950s, for no apparent reason, by an imaginative newspaperman, perhaps police-beat reporter Al Nakkula of the *Rocky Mountain News*. Reporters and editors were fond of giving crime figures catchy monikers, probably the result of seeing too many James Cagney gangster movies. The Smaldones and their crowd were no exception; they too had their handles. Clyde's brother Eugene was Checkers. Other members of the inner circle were The Harp (Paul Enrichi), The Ram (Joe Salardino), Fat Paulie (Paul Villano), and Blackie (Frank Mazza). Readers were fascinated with real-life mobsters, although Denver's version of "the mob" was much tamer and more low profile than its counterparts in big eastern cities. Offbeat nicknames, some of which actually were used within the organization, only enhanced the romance.

Clyde Smaldone, also known as Gaetan—the diminutive

form for Clyde in Italian—was born on August 27, 1906, in a row house at West Thirty-fifth Avenue and Mariposa Street, the second child and first son of Italian immigrants Raffaele and Mamie Smaldone. Eight more children (two others died in infancy) were part of the family, which made for a crowded but happy home life.

The Smaldones were adamant that their children would fit into the American way of life. It began with education. "I started at the Catholic school [Our Lady of Mount Carmel] at Thirty-sixth and Osage. Mother Cabrini was a teacher down there." Clyde often recounted an encounter with the woman who was to become a saint in the Catholic Church. "She hit me with a ruler two times on my hand because I wouldn't behave. That's when I quit going back to the school and I went to Bryant [Elementary]. You know, she's a holy woman now. She's a saint. Yeah, this hand is a good hand, the one she hit."

School didn't hold much fascination for Clyde. He quit North High School, partly to go to work to help support his family. He also quit because he disliked the football coach. Clyde said, "He knew I was a good football player, but he didn't like the Italians, so I quit when I was in the eleventh grade and I went to work in a print shop at Eighteenth and Market." He and money came together, not for the last time, because the shop printed signatures on currency for the city's largest banks. Thousands of dollars passed through the shop. "We'd run it through there to put a signature [on it]. I used to get $5 for that, and I was only making $40 a week. I was tickled to do that. I'd bring it home to Mama."

After a series of run-ins with the law for juvenile crimes, Clyde's first serious infraction went on the books in 1920 when he was thirteen years old and he and his friend Jimmy Marino got caught stealing pants. His explanation was that "we'd seen the hardware store door open. I guess they forgot to lock it. We didn't have no clothes, [so] we went in and got ourselves a pair of pants each. We both went to Golden for that." His sentence at the state industrial school in Golden, west of the city, was handed down by Judge Benjamin B. Lindsey, who was familiar with Clyde through the latter's many trips through the juvenile-court system. Lindsey believed there were no bad boys, only boys who needed straightening out. Clyde must have been, because Governor Oliver Shoup pardoned him fifteen months later. Not entirely straightened out, however. Arrests for bootlegging, reckless driving, burglaries, impersonation of a police officer, receiving stolen goods, hijacking, and brawling followed. By one calculation, Clyde rang up fourteen arrests by the time he turned twenty-four.

He was a strapping teenager, a good-looking young man with a shock of dark brown hair, dark eyes, a prominent chin, and a reputation for taking charge of the underworld business, determining how it could be run more efficiently through muscle and with ideas. As would become his style during the years when he could afford it, he dressed well. His trademark expensive cigars came later.

In his youth, Clyde and his friend Gerald Nevins, with whom he had launched his career in bootlegging during Prohibition, ran together. In their late teens, they wound up one night at the Moonlight Ranch, a speakeasy run by Mike Rossi far out on Morrison Road, southwest of the city. They flashed their liquor earnings and were quickly admitted to the club. "I think I was about seventeen," Clyde remembered. "He lets us in, me and Gerald."

They were there for the booze and gambling, but they got much more. "Here was this lady at the bar. The place was full [of] dancing. All white people except the people playing in the orchestra. And I think they had some colored people waiting on tables too. Food, moonshine, bottles to take. And she started taking off her clothes. I said to Gerald, 'Do you see what I see?' Everybody was watching. She stripped herself practically naked. I said, 'OhmyGod, they raid this place and we're in it and a broad like…' So we went back a week later and I'll be damned, here it comes again. The same thing. I finally talked to one of the guys [who] was working there. He says, 'You know who that is, Clyde?' I said, 'No.' He says, 'That's Federal Judge [J. Foster] Symes's wife.' I said, 'WHAT!?! I don't believe it.' He says, 'You believe me.'" In an ironic twist, when federal officials busted the Moonlight and its owners on liquor charges in 1925, Judge Symes, in sentencing its operators, said, "Moonlight Ranch is a stench in the nostrils of decent and respectable citizens."[1]

Clyde was careful in later years to make it clear that his running-around days with Nevins were "before I got married," which he did on August 28, 1928, in Pueblo, to Mildred Wackenreuter, a striking fashion model of Irish-German heritage who bore more than a passing resemblance to actress Barbara Stanwyck. An oft-told family story, perhaps romanticized, says Clyde spotted Mildred, who modeled under the name Mildred Walker, coming out of the Golden Eagle department store but he felt it was inappropriate to approach a lady and didn't meet her until a mutual friend introduced them some time later. The

Mildred Wackenreuter married Clyde Smaldone on August 28, 1928, and bore him two sons. She worked as a fashion model and, at times, was a single parent. © Smaldone Family Collection

couple had two sons, Eugene in 1930 and Charles in 1945. Mildred, a strong-minded woman (she loved to play poker, sometimes daily, with her group of women friends), became the disciplinarian to the two boys while Clyde pursued his dual careers in bootlegging and gambling and spent more than seventeen years of their marriage behind bars.

With mob boss Joe Roma's death by gunfire in 1933, Clyde and his brother Checkers, two of Roma's closest soldiers, became the men in charge in Denver. Clyde was twenty-seven; Checkers was twenty-three. They somehow avoided the fates of their predecessors and organized local gangs into an efficient organization with its fingers in illicit booze, gambling, bookmaking, and loansharking; its reign spanned the next forty years. Though often derided by local enforcement as small-time hoods and "the gang that couldn't shoot straight," the Smaldones and their cohorts kept a tight rein on gambling statewide and on their North Denver neighborhood, where their influence and largesse remain a topic of conversation to this day among those who lived there at the time. As Clyde recalled, "Anybody that we heard that needed something, they could come and they'd get money, we'd get 'em food. We...brought truckloads [of food] to the orphanages."

The Smaldones enjoyed a close relationship—some would say too close—with local police. So close, in fact, that when socialite Charles Boettcher II was kidnapped on February 12, 1933, and held for a $60,000 ransom, police asked Clyde for help. "I was still bootlegging, and the cops come over there to talk to me and they wanted me to be the in-between guy for the payoff. I said 'I'll do it, providing you promise me that if I know any of these guys that done it...I'll hand the money out or bring Boettcher home or whatever it is, but I don't want you to take me before a grand jury and force me to tell who done it.' They wouldn't agree to it, so I wouldn't do it." Mob boss Joe Roma also was asked to help but declined for the same reason. Without either man's assistance, police recovered Boettcher safely after he was held hostage for seventeen days on a ranch in South Dakota.

Clyde's string of misdemeanor arrests during Prohibition took a more serious turn in April 1933. In another bit of irony, it was Judge Symes, the husband of the woman an astonished Clyde and Nevins watched disrobe at the Moonlight Ranch, who sentenced Clyde and Checkers to eighteen months in federal prison for bootlegging. Clyde believed the sentencing had something to do with the boys' eye-opening trips to the Moonlight. "I guess this Judge Symes must have heard me tell somebody about his wife."

Clyde began his eighteen-month sentence at the US penitentiary in Leavenworth, Kansas, in May, but soon was transferred to El Reno, Oklahoma, where he demonstrated, in a forceful way and not for the first or last time, his concern for the underdog. "At that time, there was only three blacks, the rest of us was whites. They fed us all alike, but they had them roped off from us. They had their own shower and their own toilet and own drinking fountain. But...I noticed they weren't feeding the colored guys hardly anything. I says, 'Jesus God Almighty! What the hell's going on?' So I stalled one day and I made out that I got late and I got [in line] behind the three colored guys. They says, 'You can get ahead of them.' I says, 'No, let them go ahead.' I watched what that guy was giving them. He wasn't giving them nothing to eat. I says, 'Hey, John! What the hell's the matter? Feed them three fellows!' 'I'll feed who I want and how much I want.' I didn't say nuthin'. I ate and waited in back of the building until he got off the shift and I beat the hell outta him. I says, 'You're going to feed them guys from now on.'" They did. "They put me in the hole for that, but I did that for the colored. I didn't like to see anybody be punished for nothing. They…locked me up in a cell and they wouldn't feed me but one meal a day for three days."

Clyde's outrage over discrimination didn't subside when he caught the train back to Denver after his release from prison. "I didn't see no colored people on the train. I asked the conductor, 'Are there any colored?' He said, 'Yeah, back there.' So I went back and, ohmyGod, they were sitting on boxes and had to pee in cans and sit in the toilet the same way. They treated them like hell." He wasn't allowed to return to the all-white portion of the train, and the conductor, fearing for Clyde's safety, locked him in a bathroom until he caught a connecting train north. "Them colored people wasn't doing no harm to nobody."

Clyde and Checkers returned to Denver in 1934, but things had changed. Prohibition, the law of the land since 1920, was over, repealed in December 1933. The next step for the Smaldones, a short one, was into gambling. "Gambling was a funny thing," Clyde reminisced. "It was a damned funny thing. You had, you know, you had to learn, which we did. We could deal any kind of a game. And we started booking and we was doing all right on that, met a lot of people, traveled all over the country, met

Ova Elijah "Smiling Charlie" Stephens—he never cracked a smile—operated two of Denver's notable casinos: the Blakeland Inn, with the Smaldones, and Wolhurst. © Colorado Historical Society, *Denver Post* Historical Collection, #86.296.4145

a lot of politicians because we made pretty big money. We paid big taxes too."

The Smaldones almost immediately fell in with Ova Elijah "Smiling Charlie" Stephens, the gentlemanly kingpin of Denver gambling from the 1930s to the 1950s. Stephens was a colorful figure well known to local police. His nickname, of course, came from his dour countenance, which almost never changed. He appeared briefly in Denver in 1909 and worked as a hotel bellhop, but went back to St. Louis, his hometown. In 1926, he returned to Colorado and ran a series of gambling clubs in Colorado Springs, including the Havana Club, the Benswinger House, the Star Ranch, the Willows Club, and the Los Angeles Club. He opened the Blakeland Inn on Highway 85 (Santa Fe Drive), four miles south of the Denver suburb of Littleton, in 1933. Like all of Charlie's operations, it housed a first-rate restaurant and a show room, and offered ample opportunity for local society types to lose their money at roulette, craps, and slot machines. Newspaper advertisements encouraged tourists, "Come out to BLAKELAND, the finest night club in the West! If you don't see Blakeland your visit to Denver won't be complete. Famous for our steak and chicken dinners." It made no mention of gambling.

Adeline Tate Morris worked at the club as a dancer in the stage shows, which featured "name" acts, including dancer Donald O'Connor in his family's stage act, Judy Garland when she was one of the traveling Gumm Sisters, and, briefly, female impersonators. Adeline danced at Blakeland while she was a high school student in 1935 and 1936. "He was a really interesting character," she remembered of the short, stocky Stephens. "He was good-looking, I thought.

A newspaper advertisement for the Blakeland Inn in Littleton bragged that it featured steak and chicken dinners. It didn't mention gambling. © Adeline Tate Morris Collection

He was kind of a private person, but when we met him he was [as] sweet to us as any real uncle would be." Morris and the three other girls in the chorus were paid $10 a week for three shows a night, seven days a week.[2] She often didn't get home from Blakeland until 2:30 AM, though she recalled proudly that she never missed a day of school. Checkers and Clyde, who lived near her in North Denver, often gave her a ride home. She was taken with the Smaldones and their style. "They had an expensive taste and an expensive appreciation of things beautiful."[3]

Stephens, in partnership with gambler Leo Barnes, ran Blakeland as a restaurant and casino for only three years, closing it in 1936 after a group of clergymen complained about what was going on there. Among his employees— Clyde claimed they were partners—were the Smaldone brothers, who oversaw gambling on the casino side.

The brief Stephens-Barnes partnership had a rancorous ending: they had a falling out over Barnes's attempt to take more control of the Blakeland operation. Then came a sensational, though unsuccessful, murder attempt on Barnes. Just before 7 PM on December 8, 1936, the diminutive gambler and his wife, Pernee, climbed into their 1935 Ford sedan on the 1000 block of Grant Street, near downtown. When Barnes hit the starter, a massive black-powder explosion demolished the sedan. The explosion was so violent it drove a large piece of the windshield fifteen feet up the trunk of a nearby tree and scattered car parts in a hundred-foot radius.[4]

Miraculously, Pernee, who was blown out the passenger-side door she was about to shut, received only cuts and bruises. Leo wasn't so lucky. The charge, placed under the driver's side, drove him through the car's roof, tore away part of his left buttocks, and broke his pelvis.[5]

Several witnesses, including a woman who knew Checkers, said they saw men tinkering with Barnes's car minutes before the explosion. Police immediately arrested Stephens, Clyde and Checkers, and Eddie O'Hara, Stephens's former driver and bodyguard, who was married to murdered mobster Joe Roma's widow, Nettie.

Clyde always denied he had a hand in the bombing. "We were supposed to be involved when they blowed up some character [Barnes] that was trying to gamble in the state and Stephens didn't want him [to], so I guess that's what they did. They blowed him up, didn't kill him. He was a no good s.o.b. He was hated by a lot of guys anyhow. That woman says she saw Checkers and the others, but the only one she knew was Checkers. That broad used to come to the place on Pecos [Street]. [Barnes] was trying to move in on the gambling, Charlie Stephens's at Blakeland."

A patrolman told investigators that he saw Clyde Smaldone making a call from a neighborhood phone booth minutes before the bomb went off. Never happened, said Clyde. "I was with a detective all that day. We was out drinking. So what did they do? They arrested Checkers because this woman said Checkers was there. So, because Checkers was there, they took me and Checkers and charged us with conspiracy. This detective took the stand for me and said, 'Clyde couldn't be there. Impossible! That man was with me all day.' Judge [Henry A.] Hicks told the jury, 'That guy's lying for Clyde. Clyde had something to do with that.'" O'Hara, the fourth man indicted, was acquitted, but Clyde, Checkers, and Stephens each got

Gambler Leo Barnes testifies after his car was blown up and he was injured in a murder attempt for which Clyde and Checkers Smaldone and Charlie Stephens got ten years. © *The Denver Post*

seven to ten years in the state penitentiary for conspiracy and assault to commit murder.

It was a double whammy for Clyde, because two hours later on the same day, Judge Hicks sentenced him to four to six years at Cañon City for his part in a $450 robbery of a cigarette, candy, and popcorn truck, a sentencing that led Clyde to respond, "The police are all wrong if they think I fool around with small stuff like cigarettes and candy."[6] Clyde admitted that he was at the scene where the stolen truck got stuck in the mud in Adams County, but, he said, he only went there to help his pal Billy Lyons free the truck. "And what happened? I got stuck too." A nearby farmer, called to help pull both the popcorn truck and Clyde's green Studebaker from the muck, later identified John Lackey, Lyons, and Smaldone as the three men who robbed the truck. "Well, I got four years for that," said Clyde, even though Lyons testified that Smaldone was only doing him a favor.

Clyde went to the state penitentiary in July 1938. Checkers and Stephens followed in March 1939, after a series of appeals. As a final insult and despite his request, officers who accompanied Clyde to the prison insisted that he go in handcuffs.

He quickly became reacquainted with the prison's warden, Roy Best, whom he referred to sarcastically as "the beloved Best." The warden was known for his brutal attitude toward prisoners, striding across the prison yard in his Stetson, accompanied by his two Dobermans, Chris and Ike, and ordering prisoners to be whipped, or doing it himself. Smaldone and Best tangled almost immediately because Clyde referred to the warden as "Roy." He and

Best had known each other when Best was a member of the Colorado State Patrol, and, Clyde recalled, he used to "decorate"—his term for pay off—Best. Best dined frequently at the Smaldone family's Italian restaurant. "I used to call him Roy, and I went down to prison, me and [Checkers] went together, and I seen Roy and I said, 'Hi, Roy!' He said, 'Don't call me Roy; I'm 'warden.' He made [Checkers] a trusty; he wouldn't make me a trusty. I would never call him [warden]. I didn't give a goddamn what he done."

Best didn't hesitate to take his anger out on Clyde. "I'll tell you what he did for punishment, to me. We was building Cellhouse 6 then. He put me on the hill gang, and they handcuffed me to a wheelbarrow and another guy to the other part of the wheelbarrow. When we'd load the wheelbarrow with dirt, we'd take it up the hill and dump it in the dump. They'd have a man with a horse and a whip. If you didn't pull that stuff right, boy, they'd hit you with them whips. Roy used to whip somebody every night in that prison, and he was a thievin', no-good, rotten son of a bitch." Clyde's opinion of Best wasn't enhanced when he refused to grant Smaldone a leave to attend his father's funeral in 1938. In 1952, Best, head of Cañon City for twenty years, longer than any other warden, was suspended for violating prisoners' civil rights by flogging them and for mixing his personal finances with the prison's.

Clyde was largely self-educated. He never graduated high school, which must have bothered him because he completed an equivalency degree while he was at Leavenworth and, for good measure, earned correspondence certificates in subjects as diverse as Catholicism, metaphysics, and philosophy. He also took up painting,

Clyde Smaldone took up painting while serving time at Leavenworth Penitentiary. Among his paintings was the *Sacred Heart of Jesus*. Under prison rules he couldn't sign his work. © Smaldone Family Collection

mainly with religious themes, and painted twenty or more pictures during his stay at Leavenworth. Under prison regulations, he was not allowed to sign them.

Clyde was blessed with two extraordinary qualities: an innate intelligence—some call it "street smarts"—and an open and outgoing manner with people of all social levels, from mugs to presidents. Red Fenwick, in a lengthy three-part 1953 series on the Smaldones in *The Post*'s *Roundup* magazine, observed, "Outwardly affable, big-hearted and free-spending, Clyde and Gene [Checkers] make friends easily. They have influence and enjoy close relations with a number of high-ranking politicians, businessmen and leaders in civic and religious fields."[7]

There were other, less-publicized sides to Clyde Smaldone, sides the public, who knew him only by his frequent appearances in the city's public prints, never saw. He was an enormously gifted storyteller, able to spin stories about gold mines he had seen hidden in the Rocky Mountains when the Smaldones had stills there and how, as a sixteen-year-old, he drove for the legendary mob boss Al Capone in Chicago. One of his favorite yarns, told with a glint in his eye while he checked to see if you were buying into it, concerned his dog, Fritz. "He loved that dog," recalled his son Gene. "It was when the dog went blind and they took him up to [the veterinary school] at Fort Collins and, you know, you couldn't do anything. So, when people would ask what happened to the dog, he said, 'One morning, I was walking him in the park across the street and it was still dark out. I looked up and saw a light coming down.' He said it was an angel. 'That dog looked at the angel, and dogs can't look at an angel.' Of course, he would make a big story out of it."

Clyde so loved Fritz that when the dog died, he put it in a casket and ordered Gene to bury it in his yard in Genesee, in the foothills west of Denver. It was backbreaking work, Gene recalled, because the ground consisted largely of rocks. It took several weeks of digging to get the grave just right. Clyde checked periodically while Gene did the job, and when it was done, Clyde would gaze longingly out the bathroom window of Gene's house and say a prayer for Fritz.

Another of Clyde's favorite stories sprang from the fact that he had a full head of wavy, salt-and-pepper hair. When people would ask his secret to having such wonderful hair, he would unroll his story about how he was almost bald when he was young and how an old Indian had rubbed his own urine on his head to make his hair grow. He loved the idea that anyone might take his story seriously and perhaps try that hair-growing potion himself.[8]

A side of him known only by family members and a few friends was that he was a softie for the less fortunate. He remembered growing up in uncertain financial circumstances and gave enormous sums to charitable organizations and just plain folks. "They gave to all sorts of charities," Fenwick wrote in 1953:

> Clyde and Checkers were always good for a touch. Many destitute North Denver Italian families have found milk for the kids on their

front porches for weeks on end, thanks to the Smaldones. It is said at least five Denver boys went to college on money Clyde and Checkers put up without the boys knowing it. Orphans at several Catholic institutions in Denver have found a bonanza in the Smaldones. Each Christmas they donate quantities of athletic equipment to the homeless waifs and 'feed 'em good' at Gaetano's [the family's restaurant], West Thirty-eighth Avenue and Tejon Street.[9]

Even as a child Clyde was known for having a big heart, once stripping the blankets off his bed to give to a family that he heard was worse off than his own. He frequently invited youngsters into Gaetano's for free meals when he saw them waiting for the bus outside in the cold. He gave coal and groceries to his North Denver neighbors during the Depression and went to bat with police when neighborhood children got into trouble with the law.

One of the most touching stories the family still tells about Clyde involved a crippled orphan whom he brought home for Christmas, an act that became a tradition with him. Chuck Smaldone, Clyde's younger son, said, "They were having Christmas dinner at my Grandma Smaldone's house and everybody was there. And my dad [had] told all the family, 'You bring a wrapped gift for a nine- or ten-year-old boy.' So they all brought a gift. Dinner was supposed to be at three o'clock, and at 3:30, he isn't there. And my Aunt Genevieve said, 'You know, everything is ready. Where's Clyde?' They wouldn't start without him. All of a sudden they heard the gate close in the back and someone coming into the yard and the back door opened. They heard my dad shout, 'C'mon, I need some help!' Here he comes in with a nine-, ten-year-old boy from the orphanage in a wheelchair. They had dinner and my Aunt Gen laughed and said, 'He used to do this all the time, damn him!' My dad stayed right with him and helped him eat and everything. And then, at the end, they all piled the packages on his lap and everybody started to cry and my Aunt Gen said, 'You do this to us all the time, Clyde! Why?' 'Because this little boy never had a Christmas.'"[10]

He also was a heavy contributor to Catholic Church causes. Every year, he and Checkers would bid, sometimes several thousand dollars, for the privilege of carrying the statue of Saint Rocco through the streets of North Denver as part of the Potenza Lodge's celebration of the patron saint of their homeland. The procession was made up of youngsters carrying flowers and crosses, women and children carrying lighted candles, and black-clad women walking the seven-block route through North Denver barefoot, as penance—with the Smaldones in the position of honor, carrying the statue of Saint Rocco.

When he heard that Our Lady of Mount Carmel Church was trying to raise money to build a high school, Clyde launched a fund-raising campaign among his friends and area businessmen. "When they wanted to build a high school, Chubby Aiello, my brother [Checkers], Jimmy DeCredico, and I went around and collected money. We wouldn't take no checks and no promises. Everybody that wanted to give, they gave us cash." Eventually, they collected $50,000, a large part of it out of their own pockets, and some from fund-raising gambling nights with equipment

Clyde Smaldone, *third from left*, and his brothers paid thousands of dollars to carry the statue of St. Rocco through North Denver streets every summer. © Smaldone Family Collection

supplied by the Smaldones. The school got built. It later was demolished, an act that accelerated Clyde's estrangement from the church.

When he was in his eighties, Clyde remembered wistfully, "We fed the people and done good to the people. A lot of the police liked that. When they heard of a family in need of something, they would come and tell us, and we would take care of them. When [we had] an office at Thirty-fifth and Mariposa, the poor people would come down and say, 'We need a little money,' I told my brother-in-law Bert [Capra] and my brother Anthony, I said, 'When they come, don't you turn 'em down. We're making the money, and if you ever hear anybody needs any money or any help...They was hungry; they didn't have any money. I was glad to do it. It made me feel good. I slept good nights then, too. Even when I went to prison I used to think about that."

Yet even with charitable acts, Clyde could be calculating. Ronnie Bay, a close friend of Clyde's son Gene since childhood, recalled, "Clyde didn't do anything unless there was a deal in it. I figured that out. So my dog had died and he says, 'C'mere, I want to see you.' You never asked why; you go. He says, 'I want you to go over here. I'm going to get you a dog. I want you to pick a dog out.' And I says, 'What kind?' He says, 'Schnauzer.' Worth about $400 to $500. I says, 'Clyde, I can't afford that.' He says, 'I'm tellin' you, go get the dog. I'll take care of [the cost].' So I put 'em all in a box and go over [to the Smaldones'] and set 'em on the floor, runnin' around, a couple of 'em was peein', and Clyde says, 'Hey, look at that there, Mildred!' She says, 'Clean it up, Clyde.' So I got this one little dog and we named her Missy; it was a little female. Clyde played with it 'cuz Clyde liked dogs. Here's the deal, though. He wanted me then, when Missy was old enough, to get her bred so he could give [one to] Joe [Salardino], whose wife lost their dear dog, a schnauzer. Clyde was anything but a dummy. He was the leader. He was the guy."[11]

He also had a streetwise sense of humor. His nephew Paulie Villano lived next door to the Smaldones on West Forty-first Avenue, where Clyde loved to feed the birds and tossed seed on the driveway between the two houses. Paulie complained that bird droppings were landing on his car. The next day, Clyde spread seed all over Villano's car, which brought more birds and made Paulie even angrier.

Clyde was paroled from Cañon City by Governor Ralph Carr on December 24, 1942, for the double conviction of conspiring to blow up Barnes and hijacking the popcorn truck. He returned home to Denver after serving four years and five months. Carr, a lawyer who had defended Stephens in the 1937 trial for attempting to kill Barnes, believed Clyde didn't get a fair shake from presiding Judge Henry A. Hicks. Clyde recalled, "He knew this Judge Hicks didn't like me. Didn't like my brother, didn't like Charlie Stephens." When Carr was elected governor in 1938, he announced that he would break with the tradition of giving Christmas pardons; his friend Clyde was the only exception.

With World War II raging and the country in a patriotic

mood, the newly released Smaldone tried to join the army, but they wouldn't have him. "They told me when to come and bring my toothbrush and so forth. They...told me to come back in one week, on a Monday, and then you're going. But when I got in there, they says, 'Anybody by the name of Smaldone here?' Called me in, he says, 'Are you Clyde Smaldone?' I says, 'Yessir.' 'Were you in prison?' 'Yessir.' He says, 'Well, you can go home 'cuz we don't need nobody like you in our army.' I says, 'Okay.'"

Instead, he went to work for his mother, Mamie, who owned the struggling Tejon Bar and Cafe at 3740 Tejon Street, known to family members as "the place in the middle of the block," which they owned before Gaetano's. "My mother—they wasn't making any money—when they come down to see me in Cañon City, says the bar ain't doing nothin'. Anthony [Clyde's brother] is only taking in $15 or $16 a day. I said, 'Well, when I come home I'll come and run the place,' which I did." There he learned that with a war on, there was money to be made in the black market. It was a perfect fit, meshing Clyde's abilities at public relations and dealing with politicians—and prospering outside the law.

Eugene "Checkers" Smaldone, the toughest of the brothers—"a chill-eyed, calculating youngster"—warns a press photographer to back off after a court appearance. © *The Denver Post*

# CHAPTER SEVEN

# CHECKERS

*I wouldn't have stuck my nose in it. I can't help it; I don't believe in that stuff.*

—Clyde Smaldone

Eugene "Checkers" Smaldone didn't possess the brains or finesse of his brother Clyde, but he did know this: "Let me tell you one thing about money. Money doesn't mean anything unless you need it. When you need it, it means a lot."[1]

Four years apart in age, the brothers made their way through life with different styles. Friends and police used the word *gentleman* to describe Clyde. They more often said "mean" when referring to Checkers. Clyde was a talker; Checkers was a scrapper. In their teenage years, the latter was frequently hauled in for brawling at dance halls and saloons. He was, said one observer, "a chill-eyed, calculating youngster." As a youth he was more rugged looking than his brothers, but when he got older he wore thick, horn-rimmed glasses that gave him the appearance of a great horned owl.

Money and the pursuit of it gripped Checkers early in life. Born in Denver on July 8, 1910, the third child and second son of Raffaele and Mamie Smaldone, Checkers was a precocious car thief. His first arrest came at age fifteen in 1925, when he was caught stealing accessories from automobiles. Two years later, he and two friends, Mike Marino and Louis Santone, were arrested by Denver police and admitted that they had stolen and stripped twenty-five cars in a ten-day period, a spree that earned them a trip to the state reformatory in Buena Vista, Colorado.

Between car thefts, Checkers logged his first state Prohibition bust at age sixteen and paid a $100 fine for running booze with his brother for their father. There was an arrest for attacking a special cop at a dance where Checkers violated an area set aside for women only; one for reckless driving; another trip to the reformatory for stealing merchandise from downtown stores, his first felony conviction; and an arrest for beating up a police informant after an illicit liquor delivery. His criminal record eventually would stretch over seven decades.

He made the "big time," the front page of *The Post*, on March 3, 1931, for butting into a car chase that started in downtown and was headed for North Denver via the Twentieth Street viaduct, the main conduit to the city's Little Italy. It was at the bridge over the South Platte River that boys, acting as lookouts for the neighborhood's many bootleggers, loitered and gave would-be buyers directions to "ten for ten," ten pints for $10.

Ray Humphreys and Stanley Maus, investigators for Denver's district attorney, who had several run-ins with the Smaldones during Prohibition, were pursuing a rum-runner from Twelfth and California streets, just west of the business district, through downtown at high speed. As they crossed the viaduct, a car driven by Checkers Smaldone weaved in front of them and pinned their car against the curb. Maus fired three shots into Smaldone's car—"shooting at the tires," said Humphreys—and one

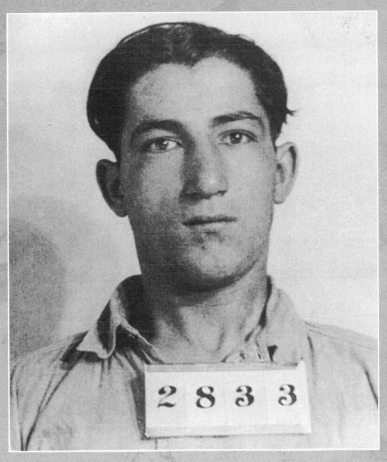

Checkers Smaldone rang up his first arrest as a fifteen-year-old for stealing auto accessories. A year later, he was caught after stealing twenty-five cars in ten days. © Denver Police Department

of the bullets passed through the car's windshield, missing Checkers's head by inches. He was fined $60, and the rumrunner got away.[2]

He did his first federal prison turn, eighteen months at Leavenworth, Kansas, in the 1933 guilty plea that prevented his parents, Raffaele and Mamie Smaldone, from going to prison for bootlegging. When he and his brother Clyde, who had also been convicted, got out in 1934, the boys went in partners with Smiling Charlie Stephens at the Blakeland Inn, an association that marked a major milestone in their careers. First, it showed them that there were enormous profits to be reaped from separating fools from their money with games of chance, including slot machines, roulette, poker, and that old Italian favorite, barbooth. Second, it got them deep into trouble when they were convicted of plotting with Stephens to take down one of his main rivals, former partner Leo Barnes.

When he went to the penitentiary in 1939 for his part in the plot, Checkers was, to everyone's surprise, a model prisoner. Clyde never got along with warden Roy Best and dutifully, but not happily, did his time. Checkers, on the other hand, almost immediately became a trusty, "one of the most trustworthy prisoners I ever had," said Best. He kept a low profile, avoiding prison politics and trouble— until, that is, a tense situation, never publicized at the time, unfolded.

Another trusty organized a prison break that included taking the warden's niece and nephew, Betty and Buddy, hostage. There are various versions of the story, but surprisingly, Checkers comes out the hero in all of them. Late one afternoon, a third trusty got hold of a revolver and invaded Best's home, shot holes in the walls, and threatened the children. Red Fenwick, writing in *The Post's Roundup* magazine almost two decades later, recounted what happened next:

> Checkers was at the prison garage only a few steps from the house. He heard the shots, walked deliberately to the kitchen door and opened it. The muzzle of the prisoner's gun met him.
>
> Cold and unmoved, Checkers said, "Take that thing outta my face. I'm not interfering with your business. You keep out of mine."
>
> With that he shoved past the convict, entered the house and, taking the two children by the hands, led them upstairs to Buddy's bedroom. For more than an hour, Checkers sat in the locked bedroom with the two children, playing checkers with each one in turn.[3]

The story was embellished later by other writers, more than one claiming that Eugene's well-known nickname grew out of that emergency game of checkers, though the handle appeared in newspaper accounts of his arrests as early as 1932.

In his own dramatic version of the incident, Clyde Smaldone, who had a soft spot for children, couldn't make up his mind how he felt about what happened. One part of him admired Checkers's courage. "By God, [that] day Gene was on the ball. He caught the one guy with the little girl. He jumped him and made him fall. The little guy before that told [Gene], 'I want you to have two other guys in there that's going to come with me. We're going to come out through the back gate and you're gonna have a car there full of gas and $500 and we're going to take the baby with us.' When [Checkers found] this guy with the baby and the gun, Gene knocked him down. The [guards] wouldn't let them guys out, they had them right there at the gate."

On the other hand, Clyde disagreed with Checkers's role in the incident. "He heard that they was going to make a prison break, and they were going to kidnap the warden's son [or] daughter, but he wasn't sure what day, and he listened to them talk and found out the day and everything. He told the warden, 'They're going to do this and this. They're going to grab the baby.' I said, 'Gene, you shouldn't have stuck your nose in that. You're wrong.' But you can figure both sides of the fence. That little girl, poor little girl, I felt sorry for her, but I wouldn't have stuck my nose in it. I can't help it; I don't believe in that stuff." It wasn't just about ratting out the other prisoners; Clyde loathed Best and never would have helped him.

Paroled with Charlie Stephens on January 11, 1943, three weeks behind Clyde, Checkers, unlike his older brother, felt no patriotic tug and made no attempt to join the military. Instead, he returned to his wife and son in North Denver and, before long, was helping run the lucrative slot-machine empire and sports parlay betting cards then coming into fashion.

Of the Smaldone cadre, Checkers was most closely aligned with the Pueblo gang and the one with the tightest ties to the Mafia, the mob equivalent of being in or out of a college fraternity. There wasn't one Mafia, a monolith like General Motors, but a loose-knit group of "families" across the country. "In organized crime, the body of the whole rarely meets," wrote Frederic D. Homer in *Guns and Garlic*. "It is better to talk about inter-group relationships in organized crime as a series of interlocking communications and alliances rather than as a confederation."[4] The Mafia demanded absolute personal loyalty and adherence to omerta, the code of silence, and Checkers fit that bill.

Checkers also was close to Pueblo mob leader Charley Blanda, with whom he frequently gambled and drank. They took fishing and hunting trips together, but their first encounter, in Pueblo's Holiday Inn—Blanda's joint, not the chain of motels—was bizarre. Joe Valley, a strapping ex-marine, survivor of the Iwo Jima landing, a Colorado Fuel & Iron millworker for forty-two years, and regarded by many as Checkers's bodyguard, met Smaldone for the first time in the late 1950s or early 1960s. Valley remembered, "They come down to see Charley [and] friends of theirs, they'd get together. This time, [Checkers] comes down, and Shorts [Steve Buccambuso], another friend of mine, we were going fishing up at Gunnison. [Checkers] was in the bar, drinking, and he heard we were going fishing. 'Hey, I'm goin' wich youse!' We looked at the guy in a suit, necktie. I said, 'Okay.' I said, 'Shorts, howinhell's he going to go fishing? He ain't got nothin'.'

"Before we leave from [the] Holiday Inn, he called his wife up in Denver to put all his fishing clothes in one of them carrying cases, a valise or something, put his fishing clothes in there and all his fishing stuff, and tie the fishing pole to the handle and ship it to Gunnison by the airplane so when we got there, it was there. That's the truth."[5]

Valley, whose real name is Joseph Valentich, disdained the bodyguard claim, preferring to say, "[Checkers] was my best drinking buddy."[6] Sometimes, the two men went on three- or four-day binges, often driving from Pueblo to Denver so Valley could deliver Checkers to his wife, Frances, who disapproved of him drinking around the house. Frequent hunting and fishing trips to Gunnison rarely went past midday and usually wound up in a local watering hole. "The next morning," Valley recalled, "he'd be pulling at my toe at 6 AM, saying, 'Get up! We gotta get going!' And we'd only been asleep since 3!"[7]

Like Clyde, Checkers kept his family life under wraps. He married Frances Cefalu in Denver on April 12, 1931, and they had one child, Eugene, born on February 5, 1936, and known as Young Eugene. Frances and her sister-in-law Mildred, Clyde's wife, were similar strong-willed women, said Clyde's son Chuck. "I was amazed when it came time to talk to lawyers or go down and bail someone out, [Frances] was exceptionally strong. Things like that didn't bother her at all."[8]

Like her sister-in-law, Frances had a taste for expensive, understated clothes. Her only accoutrements were a long, fancy cigarette holder—more of a necessity than flash because although she had only one lung, she continued to smoke, giving her a hacking smoker's cough—and a four-carat emerald-cut diamond ring. She packed a petite silver pistol in her purse. When people saw it, they would say, "Is that a gun?" She'd reply, "No, it's a cigarette lighter."[9]

Frances cooked an elaborate meal every Sunday. The rest of the week, the family ate in restaurants. The Smaldones belied the popular image of a bunch of swarthy

Smaldone family members, *from left*, Mildred, Frances, Anthony, and Checkers are cornered in a courthouse hallway by news photographers after a jury-tampering arraignment in 1953. © *The Denver Post*

gunmen and their wives taking over a restaurant. They were, said longtime Denver restaurateur Pierre Wolfe, "perfect gentlemen." He was familiar with the Smaldones because he served them often when he had a restaurant near Centennial Race Track. The night he opened his famous Quorum restaurant near the state Capitol, on October 4, 1960, it was filled with prominent citizens, including the Boettchers, Van Schaacks, Phippses, and Governor Steve McNichols. "This was a pretty gala event," Wolfe remembered. "Everybody in tuxedos. Opening night was by invitation only, and it so happened that as I was seating people and looking at the door, there stood six very familiar faces." It was the Smaldones, or, as he put it, "Whoever wasn't in the pen at the time was there."

Ever the affable host, Wolfe made room for them on opening night, though there was one moment when he felt uncomfortable. It was when Young Eugene and his gorgeous blonde girlfriend, Judy Good, entered. "She gave me a huge hug at the door and everyone saw it and the room fell silent. Some of them made remarks like, 'Uh-huh, Pierre!'" Young Eugene didn't appear to be threatened by the warm reception.

The Smaldones became regulars. "Later on, they celebrated the going-ins and the coming-outs of the Cañon City penitentiary, and they celebrated that greatly, either one going away, gave him a party, and then coming out, gave him another party. They were never out of line. They were good customers; they never complained."[10]

That was typical of the Smaldones' private lives as low-key family men. "They were just guys, always dressed nice," recalled Ronnie Bay, who practically grew up in

Clyde Smaldone's North Denver home. "When they took their coats off, they didn't have gats or guns or hand grenades."[11] At Gaetano's, the family's restaurant on the north side referred to as "the place," Clyde and Checkers would inquire of customers about the service and the food. They acted like everybody's uncles. Checkers's most frequent social transgression would occur when he drank too much scotch and insisted on singing opera, "like Caruso," said one friend who endured the arias.

But there was another, darker side to Checkers, who never lost his pugnacious streak. Cut off at the bar in a local show club, he angrily busted up the bar's glasses, threw a wad of money on the bar, and told the bartender, "This should cover it. Don't ever tell me I can't drink in here." Valley and others said they never saw Checkers tote a gun, but his extensive police record, which included a series of arrests for concealed weapons, said otherwise, and, unlike his brother Clyde, he preferred intimidation to explanation.

The gunfight at Darlene's Ice Cream Parlor, 3759 Navajo Street, is a good example. On April 13, 1970, when Checkers was fifty-nine years old, two sides met at the North Denver ice cream parlor to settle a debt owed by Joe Nuoci, twenty-nine, a bookmaker for the Smaldones with a reputation as a hothead. The scrap started earlier in the day at the Sunnyside Drug Store when Nuoci, Checkers, and Checkers's henchman, Joe "The Ram" Salardino, argued over money Nuoci owed them. They agreed to meet later at Darlene's, a few blocks away.

In the interim, Nuoci asked his friends Mike Pauldino, Darlene's owner; Tony Ciccarelli; and Bobby "The Pig" Woolverton to back him up at the sit-down. The unexpected presence of the other three men immediately rubbed Checkers the wrong way. Words were exchanged. Salardino unbuttoned his topcoat and reached into his back pocket. Assuming, correctly, that The Ram was going for a gun, Nuoci sprayed Salardino and Smaldone with Mace—nailing Ciccarelli with the overspray—and pulled his own gun, which fell to the floor. Checkers grabbed Salardino's gun and fired, hitting Nuoci in the armpit and the bullet lodged near his heart. Nuoci retrieved his gun from the floor and fired three times at Salardino but missed.

At the ensuing trial, Woolverton testified that when shots were exchanged, "That's when I headed for the door." Smaldone and Salardino were acquitted on grounds of self-defense of charges of assault with a deadly weapon, assault to murder, and two counts of conspiracy. But that wasn't the end of it. Pauldino said years later, "Checkers loved that kid [Nuoci]. He liked him better than his son. They were drunk. I yelled at both of them, 'Are you crazy!?! You're gonna get this joint closed!' I wasn't worried about anybody getting shot."[12] Pauldino went to jail rather than testify against either side in the shoot-out. "Both of them were my friends. So I refused to testify."[13] Eighteen months after the shoot-out, Smaldone was convicted of possession of a gun by a felon.

More spectacular was a late-night explosion that demolished the creamery four months later. Police contended Pauldino blew it up for the insurance; Pauldino said he had no reason to blow it up because he was making money and that it was Hispanic activists, then moving into the neighborhood, who fired it.[14]

Checkers could be cordial when he greeted guests

at Gaetano's, but he (and his brother Clyde) didn't like competition with the Smaldone gambling enterprises. Jerry Middleton, who bills himself as "Barber to the Stars" and cut hair for everyone from Las Vegas mob figures to Supreme Court Justice Byron White, was heavily involved in bookmaking in the 1960s and one day received a phone call from Checkers, inviting him to dinner at Gaetano's. He recalled thinking, *Don't worry; I know what this is all about.* As Middleton told the story, "So we have this wonderful dinner. Now dinner's over and Checkers says, 'You know, Jerry, we knew you were gambling because you used to gamble through us, but we didn't know you were [making book], and we just want to tell you that if you want to keep doing this, you're going to go through us.' And I got up from the table. I said, 'Checkers, I've got a better deal for you: it's all yours.' And that was the end of it."[15]

Checkers's nephew, Louis Smaldone, who had only a brief brush with the gangster life before going into real estate as a career, admitted, "I didn't like [Checkers]. I didn't care for him at all. His demeanor. You could see it. And he was just mean."[16] He recalled that the family's slots operation was plagued by a cheat "drilling" the machines to cause certain numbers to come up and pay jackpots. They asked operators of the machines to alert them if they saw the man in their stores. "One day, down on the old Arvada Road, this guy was in there and he was drilling a machine. They jumped in the car and we went—my dad (Fiore), Blackie Mazza, Paul Enrichi, and Checkers—we took off after this guy, and we found him in the Old Arvada area. He was going toward Louisville. Well, some way or other he got on a dirt road and he turned and he got to the very end of the dirt road and it just stopped and we caught up with him. It wasn't very, very pleasant. That's all I can say. It wasn't very pleasant."[17]

The brothers' public persona, on the other hand, was civil, especially in dealing with the police. Robert Cantwell, a Denver cop for almost thirty years who became head of the Colorado Bureau of Investigation, said, "Never once did I have an argument with them. Even when you stopped them as much as I did, [it was] 'Hi, Officer Cantwell.' They always called me by name. 'What did I do this time?' And I say, 'Well, you just ran that stop sign.' 'Okay.' They were nice, very respectful." But, he added, "I stopped them many times. It took me awhile to understand…those old days were different than it is today. They knew somebody. I never went to court on one of them. But I would go to check [and] they couldn't find [the tickets]."[18]

Checkers's blind spot was his son, Young Eugene. He refused to listen when family members and others told him his only son was involved in using and dealing drugs, a part of the underworld the Smaldones detested. It didn't help that Frances, Young Eugene's mother, doted on her only child, who was born with a malformed left hand that led him to be nicknamed Flipper. Some in the family said his embarrassment over his hand, which he tended to keep in his pocket in public, and his mother's catering to his wants led to drug problems, and his spendthrift ways helped to bring about the downfall of the family. "They gave him money like it was water," remembered his aunt Shirley Smaldone, who was married to Anthony, another of the brothers. "He got everything he ever wanted. He didn't want for anything." Checkers was a career criminal, but he loathed drugs and drug dealers. Eventually, he and the rest of the family shunned Young Eugene. The final break came when he told his son, "You get out of my life. I don't want any part of you. You're nothing but a dopehead."[19]

For Checkers—like his brother Clyde, "the product of that era once known as 'the noble experiment'"[20]—the estrangement was another setback on an increasingly rough road. The Smaldone name became synonymous with crime in Denver. One investigator said of him, "[Checkers] is not a nice guy who spends a few days a week making a little book on football games."[21] A series of arrests for gambling, increasing tensions with Clyde, and his inability to see Young Eugene for what he was would eventually overtake him.

The thriving industrial southern Colorado steel town of Pueblo was a center of Sicilian-backed criminal activity, beginning in the 1800s, and the home of the true Mafia in the state. © Colorado Historical Society, #10034470

# CHAPTER EIGHT

# PUEBLO

*Charley Blanda was kind of the big guy in Pueblo.*

—Clyde Smaldone

The "real" Mafia in Colorado was in Pueblo.

Once known as "the Pittsburgh of the West," Pueblo lived and died on the fortunes of the massive Colorado Fuel & Iron Company mills. At the click of 7 AM, day in and day out, whistles blew to alert the mills' workers that it was time to report to work. "Pennants of towering [smoke] stacks are unmistakable evidence that here industry has obtained a firm foothold in Colorado," noted a 1930s guidebook.[1] There is still a neighborhood on the south side, Bessemer, named after a steel-production process.

The southern Colorado city has cleaned up its air, and image, but in their heyday the CF&I blast furnaces produced millions of miles of rail and a noxious gray pall that hung over the town, leading to it being nicknamed Pewtown by its detractors. The collapse of US steel production in the 1980s shut down most of the mills' functions, but during its peak years, 1914 to 1929, CF&I employed 6,000 men who turned out steel wire, pipe, rail, and nails. There were plenty of jobs, which brought to town a flood of eastern Europeans, Hispanics, and Italians.

The Italians, many from Sicily, brought with them customs from the Old Country, including homemade wine and gambling, both of which got them into trouble with the law, and the age-old custom of the Black Hand, anonymous death threats from fellow countrymen warning recipients they had better pay for protection.

The first Italians to organize bootlegging and protection rackets in Pueblo on a large scale were the Danna brothers: John, Tony, Pete, and Sam. They, along with brothers Sam and Pete Carlino, ruled Pueblo's underworld in the 1920s, but the two gangs had a falling out and a string of killings ensued. When all were murdered in separate incidents, diminutive mobster Joe Roma took charge of both Denver and Pueblo, a reign that lasted until he was murdered in his living room in 1933.

With Roma's death, the mantle of "boss" in Pueblo passed, in succession, to three men: first to Charley Blanda, then to Black Jim Colletti, and, lastly to Joseph "Scotty" Spinuzzi (a brother to Nunzio, also known as Joseph, killed in 1924, during the mob wars). These three were the real deal, members of the Mafia crime syndicate. Blanda, Colletti, and Spinuzzi were firmly "connected." The Smaldones, firmly entrenched in the Denver mob, maintained friendships with all three.

Unlike the ongoing violence between Denver and Pueblo gangs in the 1920s and early 1930s, the Denver-based Smaldones and their Pueblo counterparts worked with rather than against each other, beginning in the late 1930s. The question is often raised as to whether the Smaldones reported to the Pueblo syndicate. The answer: They worked together, splitting the state into two gambling empires, north and south. In business, the Smaldones were more closely aligned with mobs in Kansas City, St. Louis, and New Orleans. They reported directly to Kansas City, where Johnny Lazia ran the mob and political boss Tom Pendergast, with Lazia's muscle, ran the city. Later, the Smaldones were close to KC mobsters Charlie Binaggio, Nick Civella, and Max "Jay" Jaben. In January 1930, Binaggio and another mob member, Tony Gizzo, were arrested in Denver for carrying concealed weapons. They were given ninety-day sentences, to be suspended if they left town within six hours, which they did. In 1950 Senate hearings on organized crime in interstate commerce, Binaggio and fellow KC gang member Walter Rainey were said to be involved in gaming in Central City, Colorado, before Binaggio was assassinated in 1950 in a double murder in Kansas City.

The Smaldones' relationship with Pueblo was based on friendships. When the Smaldones gained control of Roma's operation, they needed someone to run southern Colorado, someone they could trust. Blanda was their man.

A squat, heavyset aide to Roma, Charles J. "Charley" Blanda was born in Missouri in 1899. He stood only five foot five, weighed close to 200 pounds, wore large, thick glasses, and conjured no visions of mob "muscle," yet he had behind him a history of arrests for burglary, grand larceny, and weapons violations.

"I knew a lot of fellas down there," Clyde Smaldone recalled. "Charley Blanda was kind of the big guy in Pueblo, and Gus Salardino was down in Cañon City. He was a nice fella. And his brother, Joe. I used to see 'em a lot."

There was plenty of back and forth between the groups. When Salardino and Blanda wanted to install slot machines in Blanda's Holiday Inn and other bars around

Pueblo mob boss Charley Blanda, *left*, handcuffed to henchman Tom "Whiskers" Incerto, *right*, starts his journey to prison. Chief Deputy US Marshal N. V. Cooley, *center*, looks on. © *The Denver Post*

town, they turned to the Smaldones. Clyde was fine with that, as long as they got their cut. "I knew the sheriff down there pretty good, and they wanted to know if they could open a little gambling. I says, 'Well, Gus, I think so. I can talk with him, but, you know, you got to 'decorate.' He said, 'Well, we'll do all right.' Them guys didn't book anything. I don't think they understood the deal with booking; they never fooled with it."

All didn't go smoothly. The Salardinos slipped up on their vow that local officials would be taken care of. "[Gus] was giving his brother, Joe, the money to take care of the people that was supposed to be taken care of, and the guy come to me and says, 'What kind of guys are these? We ain't seen nothin'.' I says, 'Well, I'll straighten it out.' I went and told Gus, and Gus got his brother in there, in front of me. [Gus] says, 'What did you do with the money you was supposed to give them people?' [Joe] says, 'Well, I'm gonna give it to 'em. I want to spend it on some stuff.' We checked on him. What he done with the money, I don't know."

For the most part, each group ran its own operation, with plenty of cooperation. "We didn't have no trouble down in Pueblo. We let them run it. Charley was a nice guy. Wherever he wanted to put [slot machines], we put 'em. Charley, he made a little money, but he used to like to play barbooth. I think he lost a lot of money playing barbooth. Checkers used to go down there once in awhile, play barbooth. I was jinxed at barbooth. I lost quite a bit of money on that game."

Blanda, friendly and affable, and the Smaldone boys went way back, to the wild days of Prohibition, when all worked for Roma. In 1932, Blanda, Checkers Smaldone, and Augie Marino (the last gangster killed in the mob wars) were arrested on concealed weapons charges in Jersey City, New Jersey, when all three traveled east for a never-explained meeting that included a man later identified by police as Roma.

Later that same year, Blanda, Clyde and Checkers Smaldone, and Jim Spinelli—"henchmen of Joe Roma," said the newspapers—were stopped by Denver police at East Sixteenth Avenue and Pennsylvania Street where a search revealed four revolvers concealed in their car. "What are you fellows up to?" patrolman R. R. Richardson asked Clyde, who was at the wheel. "We're just out for a little fresh air," replied Clyde. Checkers was more confrontational. "This is my gun. I don't think you guys have any right to take it away from me. I had it in the car for protection. It's getting so it ain't safe to be out without a gun anymore."[2] All four were acquitted.

Blanda didn't escape Prohibition and his role as driver for Roma unscathed. Shortly after his arrest in New Jersey, he was shotgunned in his car thirty miles south of Pueblo. Found slumped in the front seat, bleeding from wounds in his back, neck, and shoulder, he had a ready explanation: "I was shot while I was rabbit hunting." While recuperating in the hospital, he kept a revolver comfortably stashed under his pillow in case of a follow-up hunting accident.[3]

In 1933, Blanda, Joe Salardino, John Mulay Jr., and several others were accused by Pueblo police of extorting money from gas station owners under the guise of a trade group called the Gasoline Station Owners and Dealers Association of Colorado. Police charged the association with demanding $2 to $25 a month from station owners to help improve their business. Blanda and his cohorts received seven-month jail sentences and $200 fines.

That wasn't the last Blanda saw of prison. Blanda and Tom "Whiskers" Incerto, his surly, combative bodyguard, were indicted in October 1952 by a federal grand jury in Denver for lying to federal agents and conspiring to evade income taxes. Blanda, it was charged, failed to pay income taxes of $10,692 for 1948 and 1949; Incerto forgot to tell the feds about $29,398 in taxes owed for 1946 through 1949. Their indictments were part of a statewide drive by federal and local law agencies to put a stop to organized crime with tax evasion prosecutions, a campaign that eventually swallowed up the Smaldones, Colletti, and Spinuzzi as well.

Blanda and Incerto pleaded guilty, and each was fined $5,000 and given a four-year sentence at Leavenworth, Kansas, by Judge W. Lee Knous. They didn't go quietly. Standing outside the courtroom after the sentencing, an irate Blanda shouted at his attorneys, Frederick Dickerson and Thomas Morrissey, "We coulda beat it in a trial!" Incerto, known for his hot temper, was even more animated, threatening to "bust up that camera" of a *Denver Post* photographer snapping the pair as they exited the building. "You guys persecuted me! I'm an innocent man." In a parting shot, he told a reporter, "I'm gonna pray every day I'm in jail that you have had bad luck."[4] Blanda and Incerto were paroled in 1956 after serving three years.

It wasn't all iron bars and prison walls for Blanda. He and his legion of friends were part of one of the most remembered parties in Pueblo history. The occasion was the twenty-fifth wedding anniversary celebration for Blanda and his wife, Cora, in 1948, and everybody was there. The guest list included two former governors (Teller Ammons and Ralph Carr), judges, lawyers, sheriffs, politicians, and businessmen. Not to mention Blanda's old mob buddies, including Clyde and Checkers Smaldone and their wives, Joe Salardino, Bert Capra, Louie Amidon, and Tony Colosacco.

A reporter who knew a good party when he heard about one, Red Fenwick of *The Denver Post* observed that there was "not a little elbow bending that night at the Silver Moon nighterie." He added that the party, which included champagne, wine, and an Italian dinner, set good-time Charley back $3,500. The guests pitched in and gave the happy couple 750 silver dollars (one miscreant tossed a dime in the pot) in addition to silver carving sets, candlesticks, and serving trays.[5]

Blanda, so close to Clyde Smaldone that he was godfather to Clyde's son, Chuck, died in Pueblo at age sixty-nine on February 20, 1969, a few days after suffering a stroke. His immediate successor was one of his trusted aides, Vincenzo James Colletti, known as Black Jim for his dark complexion and coal black eyes. A sturdily built Sicilian who landed in New York City as a sixteen-year-old immigrant and became a naturalized citizen in February 1920, he moved, for reasons that are unclear, from the big city to the tiny farm community of Aguilar in southern Colorado in the late 1940s and opened the Club Melody. But his real business was cheese. Colletti became a familiar figure in southern Colorado as he delivered his cheeses to customers in his pink Cadillac.

He was partners in the Colorado Cheese Company with another Mafia figure, Joe Bonanno, long identified as a mafioso. Bonanno, better known as Joe Bananas, worked out of Tucson, Arizona. The FBI regarded Colletti as the Mafia boss of Colorado, although he mostly confined his gambling and racketeering activities to the southern half of the state, leaving the Smaldones to operate in the Denver area. He kept a low profile; his only run-in with local law enforcement was a dog leash violation for which he paid a $5 fine. But he was thrust into the national spotlight on November 14, 1957, when he was one of fifty-eight mafiosi nabbed at a secret meeting at the estate of Pennsylvania mob boss Joseph Barbara Sr. near Apalachin in upstate New York.

According to Checkers Smaldone's onetime driver, Joe Valley, Spinuzzi was also at the meeting. "Scotty told me Jim Colletti couldn't get his billfold out of his pocket fast enough to show people who he was," Valley recalled.[6] "Scotty laughed when he told me about it." Among the other attendees, by some estimates as many as a hundred men, were high-profile crime figures Vito Genovese, Carlo Gambino, Joseph Profaci, and Bonanno. Law-enforcement officials believed the meeting was called to discuss pressing Mafia issues such as gambling, casinos, and drug dealing. Those apprehended in Apalachin, some of whom fled through the woods on the fifty three-acre estate throwing money and guns to the wind, claimed they were there because their pal Barbara was in ill health and they had merely dropped by to commiserate. All were eventually released because no crime had been committed, but the bust drew large publicity and alerted the American public to the extent of the Mafia's spread across the country.

In his later years, Colletti preferred to take in the sun outside his cheese store and greet the occasional well-wisher who might stop by. When he retired in 1972, the title of mob boss fell to Scotty Spinuzzi, identified by the state unit of the National Council on Crime and Delinquency as field commander for the Mafia in Colorado. Born in Pueblo in 1909, Joseph James Spinuzzi preferred to stay out of the limelight, but his fiery temper made that difficult. "[Scotty] was plain old mafioso," said John J. Koncilja Jr., a Pueblo cop from 1960 to 1997 who arrested Spinuzzi several times. "Scotty was a mean devil. He was mean. [He] was a good-sized man. He'd Sunday punch you, but he could stand up and fist fight with you too. He got to be low-key [later in life], but this guy used to get in fights, he'd pistol-whip people."[7]

Like others in his circle, Spinuzzi was arrested as a young man for a series of crimes, including Prohibition violations, receiving stolen property, safecracking, burglary, and extortion. He and his wife and son were away when a bomb or natural-gas explosion—fire officials were unable to determine precisely which—demolished their expensive Pueblo home at 2139 East Orman Avenue in 1932.

He and his brother, Tony, known as Turk, were swept up in the 1951 federal tax evasion campaign when they were accused of failing to pay $10,140.87 in 1945 income tax. The feds confiscated Turk's tavern, both men's bank accounts, Turk's 1951 Oldsmobile, and Scotty's 1950 Cadillac. The pair paid a small fine, avoiding jail time.

One of the most notorious incidents exploded in 1960, when Spinuzzi was accused of shooting to death African American pianist James Scott. Some witnesses said Spinuzzi shot him for dancing with a white woman, Scotty's date, in the Five Queens, a Pueblo nightclub

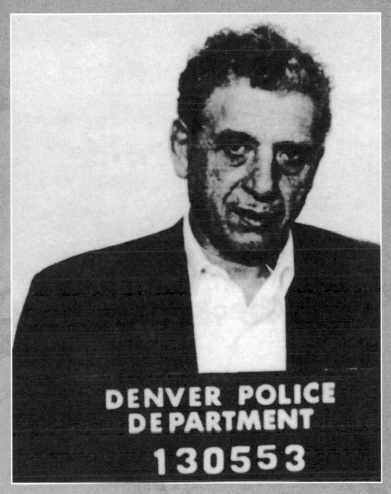

Scotty Spinuzzi, Pueblo's last confirmed Mafia boss, described by one lawman as "a mean devil," got away with murder because no one saw the bullet leave the gun. © Denver Police Department

Spinuzzi co-owned with Joe Salardino. According to witnesses, Spinuzzi told Scott, "Break it up, stop it. Don't do that. I don't like it." An argument followed, and Spinuzzi pulled a .45 and shot Scott dead. Said Koncilja, "The only reason that came to light was that the colleagues of the African American fellow were from Colorado Springs and they picked him up and were taking him out and loading him in the trunk of their car when a police car came from around the building, doing their normal patrol work, saw it, stopped them, realized it was a dead man, and put the freeze on everything."[8]

Spinuzzi went to trial for the murder but was set free on a directed verdict of not guilty by Judge George Blickhahn, who ruled that there was insufficient evidence to try him. The joke went around town that Spinuzzi got off because no one saw the bullet leave the gun. There was another, more sinister rumor that Blickhahn received a $25,000 payoff to turn the mobster loose. It was not beyond the realm of possibility. The local mob and the legal system played fast and loose with the law. The Colorado Supreme Court ruled there would be no retrial because that would constitute double jeopardy.

Koncilja advanced a theory. "The rumor was here that, and I think it's kind of substantiated by history, that the reason [the mob was] left alone by the upper echelon of law enforcement was that there was not a bank robbery in Pueblo from about 1928 or somewhere in there until probably 1968 or 1969, being the fact that this is a place to cool off, we're not gonna bother you here. You just make sure none of our [citizens] are accosted."[9] Corruption in the police department was rampant, not cleaned up until the

1970s after investigations by the Colorado Organized Crime Task Force and the Pueblo County grand jury, when dozens of officers were indicted or forced out of their jobs.[10]

Spinuzzi was arrested several times in the 1960s and 1970s on gambling charges, but his life of crime came to an end when he went to prison in 1974 on a one-year sentence, again for gambling. That same year, the federal government contended that Spinuzzi was conspiring with Bonanno to take over organized crime in Colorado. It never came to fruition, because the Pueblo mob leader died of natural causes at age sixty-five on September 6, 1975—only two months after Colletti's passing. With the two men's deaths, the Mafia's influence, beset by a changing city, increased law enforcement, and the political rise of Hispanics, vanished, ending decades of violence and corruption.

Central City went from mining ore to mining wallets when legalized gambling started in 1991. The Smaldones ran casinos in the mountain town in the late 1940s. © *The Denver Post*

# CHAPTER NINE

# CENTRAL CITY

*It wasn't such a good thing, Central City wasn't, because it was
a funny deal up there. It was all right, though; we didn't lose
any money. We can't complain.*

—Clyde Smaldone

He foresaw it. Clyde Smaldone looked far into the future
and predicted that once the government found out how
much money there was to be made in gambling, they
would get into it.

The onetime Colorado mining towns of Central City
and Black Hawk, whose glory days faded with the demise of
mining, are back digging for gold, but this time it's from the
wallets of thousands of gamblers who have been trekking
into the hills thirty-five miles west of Denver ever since the
doors swung open on limited-stakes gambling in 1991.

The history of Central City is typical of many Colorado
mining boomtowns that sprouted out of nowhere with the
discovery of gold or silver, then faded away when the riches
pinched out. John H. Gregory made the first gold strike
in 1859 midway between Central City and Black Hawk
and named it Gregory's Diggings, but it quickly became
Mountain City, and by July of that year an estimated 20,000
people flocked into the area dotted with settlements, including Nevadaville, Dog Town, and Springfield. The narrow
gulch with high mountains on either side was an unlikely

place to build a town. Central City survived a devastating fire in 1874, one that destroyed more than one hundred and fifty buildings, but it couldn't outrun the diminishing value of gold, and by 1900 the population dwindled to just over 3,000. By the 1940s, "the richest square mile on Earth" was reduced to a few hundred residents.

One of the town's historic gems (there are many, because there was no money to build new) is the Central City Opera House, financed with public subscription, which opened in 1878 and provided the flourishing mining town with civility. But as mining declined, so did the population and the need for a place to put on performances. At the end of what appeared to be its final days, the opera house was reduced to showing motion pictures. Then, in 1932, tattered and run down, it came back to life, thanks to the Central City Opera House Association, with a performance of *Camille* starring Lillian Gish. For a few weeks every summer since then, the opera house has been the scene of legitimate plays and opera productions starring big names, including Dorothy Kirsten, Sherrill Milnes, and Beverly Sills.

With the revival of the opera house came summer tourists and residents with dollars in their pockets. Then, as now, gambling seemed a good way to separate visitors from their cash. They came for the festival, but they came back for the gambling. The Smaldones, mainly Clyde, ran gambling in the little mountain town for twelve weeks in June, July, and August between 1947 and 1949. Operating out of a single small casino grandly named Monte Carlo in a storefront across Eureka Street from the opera house, the Smaldones offered craps, roulette, and slot machines to eager visitors. Nor were they alone. A local known to his fellow townspeople only as Mehl operated slot machines around town and, like the Smaldones, returned a portion of the take to civic improvements under the banner of the Flume Fund. Additionally, social clubs provided slot machines to members. Two of them combined to advertise "American Legion/VFW," which, local residents joked, meant, "American Legion and Very Few Win."

That there was gambling was no secret. William C. Russell Jr., a resident since 1937 who served, at various times, as deputy sheriff (beginning in the 1940s), councilman (1947–63), and mayor (1963–80) of the town, recalled, "One night, the city marshal and I were standing, leaning up against the gambling joint that was running, that place next to the bank. There were three men standing in the middle of the intersection [of Main and Eureka streets], on the T; one of them was the district attorney, one of them was the district attorney's man, and the third one was a sheriff. And here's this thing going full blast. Lights on, everybody in there having a big time."[1]

In the postwar era, gambling first was run by Dago Mike Mongone, who made his fortune running gambling and prostitution in another famous Colorado mining town, Leadville. Mongone was running gambling, particularly poker, in the Teller House just down the hill from the opera house, but none of the money was going back to the city.

Enter Clyde Smaldone, small businessman and city savior. It was a symbiotic relationship between the Smaldones and the onetime mining capital. With little tax income available, the town's infrastructure was in shambles. The streets were dirt and the sidewalks board planks, leftovers from the gold-rush days. In 1948, W. C. Schaus, president of the Central City Chamber of Commerce, complained, "As to sanitation, we haven't got any. Everything empties into the little creek and flows through the middle of town."[2]

Clyde Smaldone was happy to help, for a price. He went to Mongone and company. "I found out who they were and went to talk to them and I says, 'You guys made a lot of money up here and, by God, that city needs them water lines, and them kids, you didn't feed them kids, didn't buy 'em no clothes. Didn't do a damned thing except make the money and go on out. I don't know howinhell you got by with it.' They never give the city nothing, and they give nobody nothing, and I knew that when the new district attorney come in, and the new sheriff, they were men you could talk to. They said, 'You kinda got to help the city up there.' I said, 'Don't worry.' We got the places going and started feeding the kids and buying clothes, put the water line in the city, and other stuff."

Clyde, a master negotiator with a chamber-of-commerce demeanor, struck a deal with the city fathers, including Mayor John C. Jenkins Jr. and Sheriff Tom Collins, the latter a personal friend of Clyde's. "The mayor said, 'Gee, if you can help take care of some of the troubles we got up here. We ain't got no money, the houses aren't warm because we can't afford to buy stuff to keep the houses going.'

"I said, 'Leave that part to me. You can tell them to come and see me and we'll see how we do.'" The Smaldones happily kept their part of the bargain. They helped finance a new water system, paid for restoring a number of houses, and backed a lunch program for the town's schoolchildren. In return, they operated the "gambling concession" for three summers with virtually no interference from law enforcement. "If you know how to talk to people you can make money anywhere and you don't have to say, 'It's a bribe' to a governor or to an attorney," Clyde reasoned. "Them things exist okay, but there was always something the people needed, and they'd come and see you, and we was good enough to do it."

Tom Miller, who moved to Central City as a boy in 1947, remembered the Smaldones as generous fellows. As a twelve-year-old, one of his jobs was to run cigars—expensive Havana models—from Mack's Pool Hall to the Smaldones' rooms above Quiller's grocery store across Main Street. It paid well, usually a $5 tip. "You'd stick the cigar in the door and get your five bucks and go away." He worked nights cleaning the Monte Carlo. "The tables had that green felt, which I remember today as being a pool-table-type top where they did their cards and dice. If those tables were kept spotless—there was no lint on them or stuff like that—my wages were then on the tables someplace, or under the table, and so I'd make sure there wasn't anything—ANYTHING—on those tables when I was cleaning them up. I'd get a $5 or $10 bill or whatever." Even here Clyde's sense of humor played a hand. "I had to find it. It would be in a drawer or under a leg."[3]

There were no "surprise" raids on the gambling enterprises. Alerted by a phone call from El Rancho, just outside Denver, young Miller would spring into action. "Highway 6 wasn't open then, so you used to come up to El Rancho, over the top of the hill. About that area somebody would call here and say, 'The gendarmes are coming' to check things out. I don't know how I always knew these things, but I had to come down and [white out] the windows."

Clyde Smaldone (white shirt and tie, standing inside) over-sees the Monte Carlo casino in Central City in 1949. The Smaldones financed town improvements for the right to run gambling, even though it was illegal. © *The Denver Post*

When the police arrived and casually cruised the streets, they would see what appeared to be abandoned storefronts, and no gambling.

By 1949, the party was coming to an end. A new justice of the peace, Lowell Griffith, who bore a strong dislike for Mayor Jenkins (he referred to Jenkins, who owned the local hardware store, as Junk Store Johnny), came on the scene, determined to clean things up. Townspeople were outraged. Not only did they not like "outsiders" telling them how to live their lives, they had come to view the arrangement with the Smaldones as mutually beneficial. "We were happy to have them hanging around," said Russell. "Most of the people liked [gambling] because they were businesspeople [and] there was business going and the place was all lit up like a Christmas tree. Who wanted to arrest somebody who was giving you money?"[4]

Late one night, a mob formed and hung effigies of Griffith and two of his fellow do-gooders from a rope strung over Eureka Street between the bank and the drugstore, then they preceded to light the effigies on fire. "I had to go out there against the mob—I think I was fire chief, too, at the time—and tell 'em to put it out," Russell recalled. "I was afraid they'd set the town on fire. There were people waving single jacks [hammers] at people, gonna hit 'em with it. The marshal was on the side of the gamblers, and they were just having a helluva time." A full-scale riot seemed imminent. "People were locking their doors on the different shops because they were afraid they would riot, and riot in there."[5]

Clement R. Hackethal, district attorney for the area that included Gilpin County, aided Griffith in his clean-up efforts. In July 1949, Hackethal declared that dice, slot machines, and other gambling equipment were "put in mothballs." It wasn't just Central City that was affected. At the time, it was estimated that the "take" from sixty-four slot-machine locations in adjacent Jefferson County, most owned by the Smaldones, was $14,000 every two weeks, with 15 percent going to a "Youth Fund," 45 percent to the Smaldone syndicate, and 40 percent to businesses that housed the machines. Mayor Jenkins appealed to the state attorney general's office to hold off the shutdown until after the festival season, based on the argument that gambling added color and Old West atmosphere to the historic town.[6] He also noted that the Smaldones made substantial financial contributions to the community.[7]

Gambling continued through the summer of 1949, but its days were numbered. The new highway that opened between Denver and Central City/Black Hawk meant the towns were no longer so isolated, and the old "wink and a nod" from law enforcement was rapidly disappearing. "We was getting heat," said Clyde. And it wasn't just county officials; the Smaldones were beginning to feel heat from state and federal sources as well. "We know we was getting heat, and that was hurting. We had other obligations to take care of, and it wasn't worth it. But we made money, there's no question about it. We got along good up there; didn't have no trouble. After three years of that, [it] was enough for me, so we just moved out and some other guys come in and [they got arrested]. That was the end of Central City."

The Smaldone operation in Central City, which also included Checkers Smaldone, Paul Enrichi, Blackie Mazza, and Jim Spinelli, wasn't wildly successful. "It wasn't such

Denver morals squad detectives Bill Ward, *left*, and Gene Ater
look over a stash of sixty illegal slot machines confiscated at
2150 Gaylord Street in October 1948. © *The Denver Post*

a good thing, Central City wasn't, because it was a funny deal up there. It was all right, though; we didn't lose any money. We can't complain," said Clyde. "When we left, the city was a lot cleaner. I was glad we went, so we could help all them hungry kids and the other people that needed stuff and the homes that were fixed and everything. Thank the Lord for letting us go up there."

A 1951 Denver grand-jury investigation of organized gambling in Colorado claimed that Clyde and his partners reaped $25,000 to $50,000 each from Central City gaming in 1948 and 1949. Smaldone declined to confirm that, among the hundred or so other questions put to him during the investigation by Denver assistant district attorney Max D. Melville, all of which he refused to answer. Smaldone wouldn't say if it was true that the mob made $1 million a year in bookmaking.[8]

The grand-jury hearings, called to look into the syndicate run by the Smaldones, turned out to be more of a comic opera than a serious investigation. Clyde refused to answer 106 of 108 questions put to him. The sheriffs of Adams and Jefferson counties, where the Smaldones were widely known to be running barbooth and card games, were "astonished" to hear that there was gambling in their respective jurisdictions. "I haven't had any reports at all," said Adams County sheriff Homer Mayberry. "I've got a clean county. That's one thing I won't stand for— gambling."[9] Carl Enlow, the sheriff in Jefferson County, was equally surprised. "There's no gambling in my county. And there hasn't been."[10]

Even Hackethal, whose First Judicial District included Central City and who once claimed that all gambling equipment had been locked up, couldn't believe it. "I have no knowledge of it, but, as you know, I also have a private practice as well as the practice of district attorney. I am not an investigative officer." He declined to convene his own grand jury, pointing out that because no one was required to testify, it would be "a waste of time."[11]

As Clyde predicted forty years earlier, today Colorado reaps the rewards from state-supervised gambling in Central City, Black Hawk, and Cripple Creek. In 2008, the adjusted gross proceeds (total bets minus payouts) from gambling in the three towns surpassed $715.8 million.[12] Clyde offered another prediction, of more extensive gambling: "They won't make any money with a five-dollar limit on the crap games and five-dollar limit on the poker game. Five-dollar limit, for Chrissakes! They might make money because people like to play the slot machines. They go up there [for] the slot machines, but as far as the big players, they're not going to get any of that business." The state's electorate agreed, voting in November 2008 to allow the three mountain towns with gambling to vote on increasing kinds of games, raising betting limits, and increasing hours of operation. All three towns voted to do so.

President Herbert Hoover was "a wonderful man," according to Clyde Smaldone, who told Hoover he was a bootlegger when he met the president in his Brown Palace Hotel suite.
© *The Denver Post*

# Chapter Ten

# Rich and Famous

*Politicians I met were all wonderful, nice guys, like President
Hoover. What a wonderful man he was.*

—Clyde Smaldone

Clyde Smaldone was often bad with names. In his lexicon,
the federal prison in Kansas became Leavensworth; the
island prison in San Francisco Bay was Alacatraz, and New
Orleans mob boss Carlos Marcello was Mister Marcelli.

Despite his barbarisms, and unlike his brothers, he
was very adept socially, able to mix easily with the family down the block or with high-powered political figures,
even presidents. In 1932, New York governor Franklin D.
Roosevelt, making his successful run for the presidency,
set out from New York aboard The Roosevelt Special for an
8,900-mile tour to the West Coast and back, stopping along
the way to deliver speeches and meet with Democratic
officials to help solidify his already rising support.

On the afternoon of September 15, 1932, Roosevelt's
eight-car train rolled into Denver and local political types
jockeyed to get close to him. It was apparent to everyone
that in the upcoming election, then only eight weeks away,
the vigorous Roosevelt was going to unseat President
Herbert Hoover, who was taking the brunt of voters' wrath
for the ever-deepening Great Depression.

When Roosevelt's Special pulled into Union Station

Clyde Smaldone smuggled whiskey aboard The Roosevelt Special when President and Eleanor Roosevelt stopped at Denver Union Station in September 1932. © Denver Public Library, Western History Collection, Harry M. Rhoads, Rh-125

at the foot of Seventeenth Street just before 2 PM, 30,000 people were there to greet him. Among those waiting on the platform were Alva B. Adams Jr. and John T. Barnett, rivals for the Democratic nomination for US senator from Colorado; Walter Walker, Democratic state chairman; Justice Ben C. Hilliard of the Colorado Supreme Court; Governor Billy Adams; Mayor George Begole; and a gaggle of other public officials.

Earlier that day, a welcoming committee of Senator Edward P. Costigan; Raymond Miller, Democratic national committeeman; Sterling B. Lacy; and Charles D. Vail boarded Roosevelt's private car, Pioneer, during a brief stop in Limon on the plains of eastern Colorado. Already traveling with the soon-to-be-president were his wife, Eleanor; his son, James, and daughter-in-law, Betsey; and Roosevelt's daughter, Anna. Also along were newsreel crews and thirty-six newspaper correspondents.

Launched with a nineteen-gun salute from the Colorado National Guard, a parade snaked its way from the depot through downtown Denver to the Brown Palace Hotel, where Roosevelt spoke briefly from a second-floor balcony in the lobby, telling those gathered below, "I hoped to shake hands with all of you, but a man must get at least two hours sleep a night."[1]

Clyde Smaldone enjoyed rubbing elbows with powerful people but was partial to Republicans; he nevertheless saw Roosevelt's appearance as an opportunity. "I figured some way I wanted to put some whiskey on the train so they'd have some whiskey." He went to his next-door neighbor, Frank Galloway, in charge of conductors for a rival railroad, and asked if Galloway could fix it so that Clyde could slip three cases of liquor aboard the Roosevelt train, despite the fact that Prohibition was still in effect. No problem. "I had two of the redcaps working and had three cases of liquor put on the train. A case of Chickencock, Four Aces, a case, Quaker, a case. I met everyone on the train," including James A. Farley, Roosevelt's campaign manager in 1932 and 1936, whom Smaldone referred to in his offhand fashion as "Ray Farley." "They was all drinkin' that liquor."

"Time for the train to leave, I got on that train and walked around a little bit. I talked to Roosevelt for about an hour on the train. He was a nice man, Roosevelt was. A real nice man. I got off [the train] in Pueblo, but I met all the important people." His ride to Pueblo may be another of Clyde's embellishments, or, sixty years later, he may have misremembered specifics because, according to newspaper accounts of the day, after the presidential hopeful's visit to Denver, his train departed not for Pueblo, but for Cheyenne, Salt Lake City, and points west.[2]

Clyde had another brush with another president when two of his Republican judge friends—he knew a lot of judges—invited Smaldone to join them to visit with President Herbert Hoover for twenty minutes in his suite at the Brown Palace Hotel.

It was a bizarre scene. "[Judge] Black called me up and said, 'Say, Clyde, would you like to see the president?' I said, 'Sure. He's a nice man, I hear.' We walked [into the hotel] and here were [Secret Service] men all over. 'Where youse going?' 'We're gonna go up and see the president.' 'You got a reserved time?' 'Yes.' They said [looking at Smaldone], 'How about him?' 'Oh, we brought him with us, figuring you let him come with us.'"

Having breached the first line of bodyguards, they were escorted up in the elevator, frisked and questioned again, and then led in to meet Hoover. Small talk ensued. "He talked to the two judges and then he says, 'What do you do, Smaldone?' I said, 'I don't want to lie to you, Mr. President. I'm a bootlegger.' I thought them two judges was going to die. But the president got up and started laughing. He said, 'There are some honest men in this world!' When we left, he shook my hand."

Clyde met Harry Truman years before he became president. It's no secret that as a rising young politician in Missouri, Truman had close ties with Kansas City political boss Tom Pendergast. "Truman played a key role in maintaining the Pendergast control of life in Jackson County [Missouri] after 1926. He not only knew of the machine's illegalities, but also participated in some of them. Truman was a practical man and used the machine to get what he wanted," Richard Lawrence Miller wrote in *Truman: The Rise to Power*.[3] With Pendergast's support, he was elected a commissioner for Jackson County, which included Kansas City, then became a US senator. When Truman first went to the US Senate, colleagues referred to him as "the senator from Pendergast."[4]

Clyde met Truman very early in the future president's career, shortly after his failures as a farmer, wildcatter, and haberdasher. "I knew Truman when he didn't have money to eat. He was an errand boy for Mr. Prendergast. When I'd go to Kansas City, I used to see Truman quite a bit when he was nothing. I knew the Italians in the Democratic Party used to give him $125 a week. Prendergast liked to play the college football teams, and he sent Truman up to the

Chesterfield Club in downtown Kansas City. Give Truman the money, go up and bet on the games.

"He should have gotten Prendergast out of prison [where he was serving time for income tax evasion] when he was vice president. And before he become president, Prendergast died. That was a shame. He could have turned Prendergast loose; he had the power." When Pendergast died in 1945, Vice President Truman flew on a military plane from Washington, DC, to Kansas City to attend the funeral, causing multiple raised eyebrows. Truman's typical caustic response: "Everybody said I shouldn't go to the funeral. What kind of a man...wouldn't go to his friend's funeral because he'd be criticized for it?"[5]

A string of Colorado governors were friends of Clyde's too. He was particularly close to Ralph Carr, governor from 1939 to 1943, whom he described as "a very dear friend." Like Smaldone, Carr disliked mistreatment of minorities, which helped cost him his political career. When President Roosevelt ordered Japanese Americans interned in Colorado during World War II, Carr encouraged his fellow citizens, many of whom didn't want the internees in the state, to treat the newcomers with respect. He spoke out against incarcerating American citizens of Japanese ancestry.

Their friendship dated to 1937, when Carr defended Charlie Stephens, Clyde Smaldone's coconspirator in the unsuccessful car bombing of gambler Leo Barnes, and Carr got a firsthand look at the way Judge Henry A. Hicks rode roughshod over the defendants. Ironically, when Carr was named US attorney for Colorado in 1929, one of his first bits of business had been to prosecute the Smaldones for

Colorado governor Ralph Carr—" a very dear friend," said Clyde Smaldone—knew the Smaldones as a prosecutor and, later, pardoned Clyde from Cañon City in 1942. © *The Denver Post*

Prohibition violations. But he felt Smaldone got a bad deal in his dual sentencing in 1937 for the attempted Barnes assassination and the theft of a popcorn and cigarette truck, so, in 1942, he pardoned Clyde. "He come down to Cañon City and said, 'Clyde, I'm gonna send for you in two or three days 'cuz I'm going to pardon you and take that off your record, these two deals you got, because that Judge Hicks was poison. He didn't give you a fair trial. You done nuthin' wrong.'" Their friendship went even further, said Clyde. The two attended the wedding of Pueblo mob boss Charley Blanda's daughter together, driven there by Carr's chauffeur. "A fine man, Carr was, and we stood at the wedding."

All in all, Clyde admired politicians. In his eyes, they were "nice guys." "Politicians I met were all wonderful, nice guys, like President Hoover. What a wonderful man he was." Clyde claimed many other high-ranking friendships, with governors Clarence Morley and Dan Thornton; Denver mayor Ben Stapleton; Ku Klux Klan leader John Galen Locke; and mob bosses Vito Genovese, Frank Costello, Al Capone, and, in particular, Carlos Marcello, who ran the rackets in New Orleans and elsewhere in Louisiana.

The Smaldones and Marcello became close friends when the New Orleans boss was banned from the horse racetrack there because of his gambling connections. Clyde sent his nephew Paulie Villano out to the track to talk with federal inspectors, whom they knew from Denver, to convince them to lift the ban on Marcello. It worked (not incidentally because, Clyde recalled, he gave them "presents, something for their wives, little odds and ends"), for which Marcello was very grateful. "Mr. Marcelli wanted to give [Checkers] and I one-third if we'd come down in Louisiana and help him with the games and help the family down there. I felt like going, but Gene didn't want to go, so we said no."

The close ties between the two families included the Smaldones laying off bets in New Orleans and Marcello trying to give Clyde a religious statue from his vast collection. "He wanted to give me a beautiful thing to put in my house, a Catholic statue, and I wouldn't take it. He wanted to give me a beautiful, beautiful statue of Christ. His whole house: all statues of Christ and the apostles. He had so many nice things. I said, 'No, I can't take it, Mr. Marcelli,' but now I'm sorry. It was the most beautiful thing you ever seen."

Clyde scoffed at the notion circulated among assassination buffs that Marcello, who died in 1993, had a hand in President John F. Kennedy's death. It was Clyde's business associate Frank Curley who told him, "The two men who killed the two [Kennedy] sons, they was nobody. Nobody hired 'em to do it. These two crazy dingbats killed the two Kennedy brothers. It was the work of God."

Neither beautiful nor nice in Smaldone's eyes were the Kennedys, whom he despised, beginning with Joseph P. It has long been accepted that Joseph Kennedy's fortune was rooted in bootlegging. Seymour Hersh referred to it briefly in his 1997 book, *The Dark Side of Camelot*:

> The most direct assertion of Kennedy's involvement in bootlegging came from Frank Costello, the most powerful Mafia boss of the 1940s and

1950s, who sought in his later years to cast himself as a successful businessman. Costello...con-
fided that he and Kennedy had been "partners" in
the bootleg business during Prohibition—a partnership that began, Costello said, after Kennedy
sought him out and asked for his help.[6]

Clyde Smaldone knew more than that, thanks to his
connections in the New York mob, including to Genovese
and Costello. Even in the late 1930s, Clyde said, Kennedy
was making big profits off liquor. Prior to the United
States' entry into World War II, the US government was
sending aid to England, and, said Clyde, "[Kennedy] knew
these...ships were coming back empty. They went to
England loaded with food, medicine, everything because
they were fighting Germany then. Kennedy sent word to
Frank Costello if he could get $3 million for him. Vito
Genovese [ran] the longshoremen's union, so they gave
him the $3 million and he gave the money to Kennedy.
He used the $3 million and loaded all those boats coming
home empty, brought 'em to New York. [He was buying
whiskey in Ireland], buying whiskey, buying whiskey, sent
it to the United States. They made so much money you
couldn't believe it. Say a case of whiskey was $20. They'd
put out $10 for Kennedy."

Smaldone's enmity extended to Joe Kennedy's sons,
Jack and Robert. It was Robert who spearheaded the federal government's campaign against organized crime when
he pushed Congress into passing three federal acts in
1961 that crippled interstate gambling. "Bobby Kennedy
hated gamblers," David G. Schwartz wrote in *Cutting the*

*Wire*. "Not your $2-a-horse bettors, or guys who played poker once a week to unwind. For Kennedy, a 'gambler' meant boss gamblers, the shadowy men who controlled the action, running illegal numbers games or taking off-the-books bets on legal horse racing."[7]

A religious and moral man despite his professional life of bootlegging and gambling, Clyde was appalled by the extramarital antics of Jack Kennedy. "There was a bad, bad family. That was a regular whorehouse when [Jack Kennedy] was president. Broads up there, they had parties, drunks."

In addition to Genovese and Costello, Clyde had other, more colorful mob friendships. He became acquainted with Chicago mob overlord Al Capone during the Prohibition era, when the Smaldones were running whiskey from Canada to Colorado. He recalled meeting one of Capone's henchmen and discussing the high cost of good liquor. "[He] was going to talk to Al. And [he] says, 'Come back in about a week, Clyde, and we'll see whatthehell we can work out. Is there any place we can load down there?' I says, 'Hell, it's right across the Mississippi, and Burlington, Iowa, is right there.' He said, 'You could fix somebody to take care of the load if we loaded it ahead of time so it'll be ready for you when you come?' 'Yeah.' So I went and seen this bootlegger and told him about the deal. He says, 'Yeah, I can fix it with the guys. Just pull them right in the garage, you'll have your overload springs on. You bring them springs up and we'll overload the bonded whiskey you want to put in the car.' They talked to Al about it. I was paying 66 [dollars] in Canada, and Al got it for me for 35 a case. He'd bring it down, we'd load it and take it out. I sold a lot of that.'

Although they weren't close friends, Clyde and Capone met on three or four other occasions, including just before Capone's death. In Smaldone's eyes, Capone, who helped him obtain cheaper whiskey, was a generous man, not a killer and criminal organizer. "I didn't see him again until the country went wet. And that's when they took him on charges of tax evasion, them dirty...And that man spent all that money feeding the poor in Illinois for soup lines and everything." Capone was released from Alcatraz in 1939 and went home to his estate in Florida, where he died in 1947. Clyde visited him shortly before his death. "He was glad to see me. He even asked me, 'How do you stand on money?' I said, 'It's all right.' He gave me the name of a fella and says, 'If you ever need anything or need any money, you go see him. I'm going to put a mark on this so you can show him this.' Well, I don't have that anymore. I tore it up and burned it.

"They told Al he had syphilis, and that's a damned lie; he never had syphilis. I think his heart was broken more than anything. I snuck down and got to see him a week before he died. Nobody knew when I went and nobody knew when I come back except him and I and one other fella."

Somebody else knew, because when he got back to Denver, an agent from the Federal Bureau of Investigation came calling. "Somehow, some way, one of them FBI must have knew me and told agents over here and they called me and we met someplace. He said, 'Were you down in Florida?' 'Yeah.' 'You see anybody down there?' 'I don't remember going to see anybody. I just stopped, went a few places, a few bars. I figured that was my vacation.'"

The agent persisted.

"'Somebody told me you was…You went down to see Al.' 'Me? Al? I don't know Al, Al don't know me either. Why would I go down and see him?' That was the end of that."

Capone died on January 25, 1947. The official cause of death was a heart attack. Clyde recalled his friend simply: "God knows he was a good man to me and he was a good man to the people. And somebody had to bootleg, and they all wanted it, so why not put some of that money to good?"

Friendship, trust, and loyalty went hand in hand with Clyde Smaldone. In the fashion of omerta, the mob code of silence, his memory would fail him at convenient moments. So it was that even late in his life, Clyde declined to talk about some of those he called friends. "It was a long time ago, yes. I knew a lot of them, but I can't remember their names. I don't care who he was. We had friends every place in the United States. Everybody we had to know, we knew."

Clyde, *right*, and his lawyer Frank Mancini leave the federal court-house in Denver in 1953. The Smaldones reached the pinnacle of their gambling power in the early 1950s. © *The Denver Post*

# THE HEIGHTS

*I was the only one in the city of Denver who could get all the*
*liquor and whiskey and beer I wanted, and then the food. I stood*
*open seven days a week, and we started making big money.*
*The place done real good.*

—Clyde Smaldone

For the Smaldones, especially Clyde, World War II and
its aftermath marked a turning point in their careers in
crime. After he left the prison at Cañon City and was
turned down for military service because of his criminal
record, Smaldone returned to North Denver in December
1942, the depths of the war, to help his family run the
struggling Tejon Bar and Cafe. Things were worse than he
thought. His mother, Mamie, who owned the bar, and his
brother Anthony were making less than $20 a day. There
was a war on, as a popular poster reminded Americans.

"Things were tough, everything was rationed," Clyde
remembered. But, by a stroke of luck, the answer to their
problems walked into the little bar one day in the form
of Frank Curley, a nephew of notorious Massachusetts
politician James Curley and a Franklin Roosevelt appoin-
tee. "Frank Curley came in the bar. He was in charge of
[government] rationing in seven states. He come by every
time he went up to Wyoming to bring money for the army
posts up there. He'd stop with them Jeeps loaded with

cash. But he was in the Cadillac, had a colored driver, and had the radio and everything in there to talk to anybody he wanted. Then we got pretty personal. He used to bring his wife to the bar and we'd drink."

Clyde's outgoing personality and political acumen once again served him well. "He took a liking to me. He used to come over there [and] he'd say, 'Clyde, you getting liquor?' I said, 'Yeah, I'm getting liquor.' He said, 'That's the only thing that I ain't got rationing. I got food, tobacco, cigarettes, automobiles, this and that, gasoline. Clyde, you want any of that stuff, I can get it.'"

Clyde Smaldone knew opportunity when it knocked on his saloon door. A thriving black market in rationed goods was rampant across the country. Clyde wanted all those items—which were in short supply and legally obtainable by the public only with coupons or rationing stamps—and he wanted more. The grand prize was gasoline. Rationing of gasoline, begun in 1942, was designed to discourage driving and save wear on tires after Japan cut off US rubber imports from Southeast Asia. Allocations were based on need. "A" windshield stickers went to those with nonessential needs (visiting friends and so on) and were good for three or four gallons a week, and essential, or "B," coupons, given to war industry workers, were good for eight gallons a week. "C" coupons went to physicians, ministers, mail carriers, and railroad workers. Congressional members took care of their own needs by giving themselves "X" stickers, good for unlimited fill-ups.

In May 1943, rationing went into effect for practically everything else: canned goods, shoes, clothing. The joke was on the American public because while workers were taking home large paychecks, there were limited goods to spend the money on. Particularly scarce were butter, sugar, and meat. A complicated point system was imposed by the federal Office of Price Administration, one in which a one-pound steak, for example, cost twelve points, and a pound of butter was sixteen points. The government made it clear that the stamps weren't to be passed around. Each book came with a warning: "This book is the property of the United States Government. It is unlawful to sell or give it to any other person or to use it or permit anyone else to use it, except to obtain rationed goods for the person to whom it was issued. Persons who violate Rationing Regulations are subject to $10,000 fine or imprisonment, or both." This didn't dissuade Clyde, who went for the big prize. "I told him, 'I can use some stamps for my friends in the gasoline business.' He gave me stamps and I gave them to my friends. I coulda made a lot of money 'cuz I coulda sold it." For Clyde, the goodwill—and the paybacks that would follow—were at least as important as whatever cash he might turn from selling stamps.

Clyde's wife, Mildred, became a conduit for the gas stamps. "A friend of mine in California said he sure could use some stamps, and I talked to Frank and he said, 'I'll get them for you, but you don't drive that car to California. A woman they won't bother. They see men, they'll stop and shake everything down.'" Curley suggested Clyde's wife as the courier.

"'Your wife can drive good?' 'Yeah.' 'She got a little boy?' 'Yeah.' 'Let them go. I'll give you so many thousand gallons of stamps.'"

The little boy was the Smaldones' son Gene. Mildred,

Gene Smaldone and his mother, Mildred, made drive trips to California during World War II to deliver black-market gasoline coupons destined for Hollywood stars. "I thought we were on vacation," said Gene. © Smaldone Family Collection

her mother, and twelve-year-old Gene made three or four trips between Denver and Los Angeles to drop the gas stamps with a station owner Clyde called, in his fractured way, Pizzacheta or Pitz. His last name actually was Pizzichino; his uncle, Frank, was a cop in Denver. "I thought we were going on vacation," Gene recalled years later.[1] The filling station became a gathering place for Hollywood stars, including a young actor who became California governor and then president, Ronald Reagan. "They knew about Pitz having extra gas. They all used to go down there and get gasoline. [Mildred] met Frank Sinatra, met a lot of stars. She was glad, too, because she got to meet everybody."

The only thing Curley didn't ration was liquor, but Clyde knew where to get that. Although in short supply, alcohol was not rationed. Smaldone knew people. "My friend [Angelo "Brownie" Distasi], he was the boss of Calvert. Calvert was a big seller then. My wife's sister, Margaret...married the man who was in charge of the [Blatz] beer corporation here. Between the two of them, they sold Blatz, the biggest [beer] seller, and Calvert, the biggest [whiskey] seller. This Frank Curley had some other friends, and I used to get him ten, fifteen cases of beer he wanted to give to others. I'd say, 'Do they pay?' 'Yeah, they'll pay.' 'If not, I'll pay for 'em and give you the damned things.' 'No, Clyde, I'll do it the way I want to do it.'

"He was doing it for friendship. I could get that stuff. Everything any of my friends wanted, food stamps, everything. I never made a nickel, and he didn't either. He was really a religious man. He knew what he was doing was wrong. I did too."

Business picked up at the bar immediately. "I was the only one in the city of Denver who could get all the liquor and whiskey and beer I wanted, and then the food. I stood open seven days a week, and we started making big money. The place done real good. Made more money there than Gaetano's made. Everything was happy."

It did even better when Clyde and Checkers began dealing in football parlay cards, where bettors could wager as little as $1 to pick college football and basketball games each week. Pro football was still in its juvenile stages and was not the attraction for fans or gamblers it later became. To win, bettors were required to pick three or more teams to win by more than the point spread. Odds varied from 8–1 to 100–1, depending on the number of games played. "That was the start of us on gambling [with parlay cards and barbooth instead of only slot machines]," said Clyde. "Then Checkers and I, we got places. We ran gambling, barbooth, and loan-sharking."

It was the best of times. Though they continued to operate into the early 1980s, the high-water mark for the Smaldone empire was the years between 1946 and 1953. The mob's gaming and loan-sharking activities were reaping huge rewards, as much as $1 million a year by some law-enforcement estimates. "Bookmaking on sporting events is organized crime's number one source of income," said a 1971 report by the Organized Crime Unit of the Denver district attorney's office.[3]

The widespread Smaldone organization had nickel-plated slot machines in drugstores, bars, and clubs all over the state. They owned 585 of them by Clyde's account, and they were legal by buying a $100 federal tax stamp—but

Football parlay cards became the organization's gambling bread and butter in the 1960s. Bettors could pick three or more games for as little as $1. © Denver Police Department

# How to Play Barbooth

Also known as *barbuit*, *barbotte*, or *barbudi*, the dice game barbooth originated in the Middle East and became very popular among Greeks, Jews, and Italians, who brought it to the United States.

It's a simple, fast-paced game played with a pair of dice. There are four winning numbers, 3-3, 5-5, 6-6, and 6-5, and four losing numbers, 1-1, 2-2, 4-4, and 1-2. All other combinations are meaningless. Thus, the odds of winning are fifty-fifty.

The person with the dice is known as the shooter, and the next person to shoot is called the come-out man. The shooter tosses the dice, and the come-out man puts up a stake, which the shooter can cover all or part of. The other players around the table make side bets against each other on whether the shooter will throw winning or losing numbers. As long as the shooter wins, loses with a 1-2, or the come-out man wins with a 5-6, the players' roles remain unchanged for the next round. Otherwise, the come-out man becomes the shooter.

When he loses, the shooter passes the dice and the "box," a cup containing the dice, to the next player and the game continues.

As played in Colorado, there is no house, which nevertheless charges players a pinch, or rake-off, to stay in the game. The pinch is collected every twenty or thirty minutes.[2]

illegal under state law, which wasn't enforced.

Barbooth games, run by the Smaldones and their associates in metro Denver and Pueblo, became an almost nightly event. The dice game was brought over from Italy by immigrants and was a leading source of recreation in the Italian community. Unlike craps, a better-known dice game, there was no house. Players played against each other but periodically paid a small amount, called the pinch, to the organizers to stay in the game. If a player ran out of money, the Smaldones were happy to make him a loan, at exorbitant rates. A $100 loan advanced on Monday, for example, required $5 a day in interest, a $125 payback by Friday, and it grew from there if unpaid. A high-risk customer might pay 150 percent in interest.

It was a river of cash. Both of Clyde's sons recall their father digging into his pockets and extracting fat rolls of bills at the end of the day. "He had different pockets, different accounts," remembered Clyde's son Chuck. "This would be gambling money, this would be loan money, and he'd set them down on the table and in different piles, and there was always a big wad, sometimes four, five, six, seven thousand dollars, maybe more."[4]

It was a bonanza no three-year-old could resist. "The Happy Home Bakery used to come around to the house," Chuck recalled. "My mom was in the kitchen and she had the water going and she didn't hear the bell, so he came in and he said, 'Happy Home Baker!' I came to the door and he said, 'Little boy, go get your mom.'

"I said, 'Well, I want those powdered-sugar donuts. They're my favorite.' They were 60 cents or whatever they were back then. I had no concept...I knew that money was money but not value, so I just grabbed a handful, probably two or three thousand dollars. I handed it to the Happy Home man. His mouth dropped open and he said, 'Mrs. Smaldone!' Back then, people were honest. My mom came and she laughed when he said, 'That is too much for the donuts.'"[5]

Mother had her moments with the cash flow too. "Dad used to stuff his pockets," Chuck said. "A couple of times, she'd go down to the washing machine and she'd open it up and there'd be money floating around. One time, she put it on the clothesline, before she had a dryer. There was all this money hanging out there and she sat out and sat on a chair and waited until it dried."[6]

Beginning in the 1930s, Clyde and Checkers enjoyed an amicable relationship with law enforcement by, as Clyde put it so elegantly, "decorating the mahogany." In postwar Denver, bribery was still a fact of life, although less blatant than during Prohibition. As an example, in 1946, members of the Denver Police Department campaigned to get a measure on the ballot to improve their pensions. Listed among the dozen persons who contributed to the successful campaign—"friends to whom we wish to extend our sincere thanks and appreciation"—were Clyde and Eugene Smaldone.[7] The measure passed by 9,000 votes.

The Smaldones' operations were running full tilt, yet barbooth games in Denver and Adams counties and slot machines weren't enough. They also were making book, taking bets by telephone on horse racing and other sporting events. And anyone who ran large-scale gambling in the city cleared it with them. Even in Five Points, Knockout Brown came to them to get permission to run games in the largely African American neighborhood. "We had it fixed that no one would bother him," said Clyde.

From 1947 to 1949, Clyde had the sweetheart deal with officials in the mountain town of Central City to open a casino. They made contributions to the city's needs in exchange for gambling rights. Their slot machines also were spread over Adams and Jefferson counties, Denver, and in Pueblo, although Clyde noted, "We let them have theirs," loaning Charley Blanda and his group fifty machines so they wouldn't have to buy them. "Took in a lot of money, gave a lot of money away. We was good."

In 1947, the Tejon Bar was thriving, so much so that Clyde decided to buy the drugstore and meat market on the corner of West Thirty-eighth Avenue and Tejon Street, just up the block, and open an Italian restaurant, which he named Gaetano's, after his paternal grandfather. "I borrowed $22,000 from [my friend] Jerry Losasso to pay it off. We paid it off with football cards." It was an instant success, the best Italian eatery in town, some said. Patrons lined up to partake of the food, most of it prepared by Mamie Smaldone and other family members. It was the family's pride and joy, described as so well maintained you could eat off the floor, which helped keep the city inspectors off their backs. It also became the epicenter of the family's gaming empire.

Times were good. But they were about to come to a halt, thanks to two unimpeachable anticrime crusaders of a kind the Smaldones hadn't encountered before, not even in their days as bootleggers. The mob began to feel the heat in 1950 when, in Clyde's words, "This one district attorney, he come and raided one of the places, but we got the tip ahead of time. Didn't do him no good, see, but I

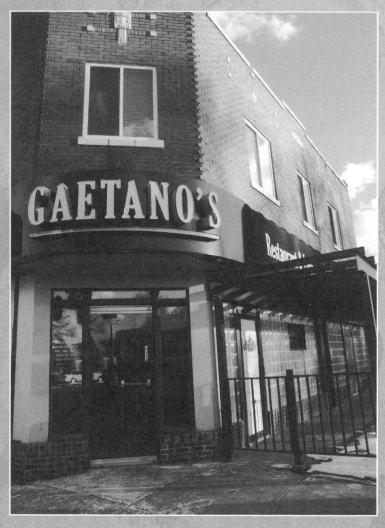

Gaetano's restaurant, known as "the place" to the family, opened in 1948 at West Thirty-eighth Avenue and Tejon Street, and remains a popular North Denver Italian eatery. © Molly Kreck

knew he was going to [come back] afterwards." He quickly disposed of the machines, selling all 585 of them to Las Vegas interests, including Bugsy Siegel. The last load was trucked out of town less than two hours ahead of the law. "We got moved out just in time."

Crusading government attorneys Charles Vigil, *left*, and Max Melville teamed up in the early 1950s to launch a drive against gambling, targeting the Smaldone syndicate. © *The Denver Post*

# CHAPTER TWELVE

# 1953

*The next time you shoot my picture, I'm going to punch you in the nose.*

—Clyde Smaldone

The Country Mouse and the City Mouse, Charles S. Vigil and Max D. Melville, were as different as two lawyers, or two people, could be.

Vigil was the thirteenth child born into a Hispanic family in Trinidad, Colorado. His father died when Charles was three, his mother when he was seven. He worked his way through law school at the University of Colorado, spent three years in the Coast Guard during World War II, and then settled in as an assistant district attorney in Trinidad.

Out of nowhere, President Harry Truman selected him in October 1951 to be US district attorney for Colorado. Vigil immediately launched a spectacular, if brief, public legal career. His high appointment was so rare for a Hispanic, he felt compelled to tell reporters at his first press conference, "That name is pronounced as though it were spelled 'V-hill.'" He was only thirty-nine years old.

Melville, on the other hand, was the son of a lawyer who served as Colorado's deputy attorney general. He attended upper-crust Denver East High School, got his law degree from the University of Denver and his doctorate from Yale University, and became a noted writer and lecturer on law. His *Criminal Law in Colorado* was a must-read for law students.

In September 1951, Governor Dan Thornton named him to the Colorado Crime Commission, known as the "little Kefauver" committee after the federal hearings into organized crime then going on in Washington, DC, and headed by Senator Estes Kefauver of Tennessee. The state commission was charged with ferreting out undercover crime, including gambling, drug trafficking, and slot machines. Colorado had seen many crime clean-up campaigns come and go with little effect, but these guys were serious. The city's newspapers, particularly *The Post*, whose editor Palmer Hoyt made crime-busting a centerpiece of its news coverage, kept up a drumbeat on page one.

Vigil was regarded by his peers as a plodding and patient man. Melville was a gruff-talking, high-profile dynamo and a onetime sportswriter for the *Rocky Mountain News* who somehow kept going simultaneous careers as practicing attorney, teacher, lecturer, and author. He also enjoyed playing billiards in a downtown pool hall almost every Saturday for twenty years with lawyer pals Duke Dunbar and John Carroll.

As different as their backgrounds and temperaments were, the two men combined forces to mastermind the downfall of the Smaldone crime syndicate under the bright light of intense media coverage. Vigil was on the job only two weeks in late 1951 when he ordered his staff to begin collecting $10,000 in bootlegging fines unpaid since Prohibition days. Among his targets: Clyde and Checkers Smaldone, who failed to pay $1,000 each as part of their convictions in 1933. The two eventually paid their fines, stringing it out at $100 a month.

Melville was even more aggressive. When he joined the crime commission, he made clear his attitude toward lawbreakers: "Keep 'em busy picking up their teeth."

With the close partnership of Vigil and Melville, the Smaldone organization was hammered on all sides by federal, state, and local law enforcement. Melville and Vigil first went after the widespread use of slot machines, and then began using income tax laws to nibble away at the organization's members. Smaldone aides Blackie Mazza and Paul Enrichi were convicted in 1951 for evasion of state income taxes. At the same time, Clyde and Checkers Smaldone refused to answer questions put to them during a special Denver grand jury investigation on gambling, led by Melville. Checkers declined because "his answers might tend to incriminate him," while Clyde gave his name and address but, reading carefully from a typewritten statement, replied, "Same answer," which meant no answer, to 106 other questions about his life and business dealings. Among the questions he declined to answer were whether he had a brother named Checkers and whether Mamie Smaldone was his mother. Melville wanted both brothers cited for contempt for their refusals, but Judge Joseph E. Cook ruled that the Denver grand jury had no jurisdiction in the case because the alleged violations took place in Jefferson and Adams counties, outside the city.

Vigil kept up the pressure in 1952 when he convened a federal grand jury to look into syndicated crime in Colorado. Two law-enforcement officials were indicted for lying about payoffs they received to ignore gambling in their counties. The issue of the Smaldones' relationships with politicians and police in Central City was dragged out again. Clyde's nerves were becoming frayed by his repeated courtroom appearances. While testifying for Mazza in his tax-evasion trial, Smaldone went after a *Post* photographer in a hallway outside the courtroom, snapping, "The next time you shoot my picture, I'm going to punch you in the nose." He cocked his arm as if to throw a punch, but his lawyer, Thomas Morrissey, interceded. Morrissey, Fred Dickerson, and Anthony Zarlengo were partners in a politically well-connected law firm that frequently defended mob members.

Less than a year later, Clyde, Checkers, and twenty-nine others were hauled into court over an apparently fixed dice game at a pool hall at 7057 Federal Boulevard. Philip Van Cise, legendary Colorado bunco crime fighter from the 1920s who broke up the infamous Lou Blonger gang, was brought in as special prosecutor. He received the extraordinary sum of $4,500 to help convict the Smaldones. Even he wasn't able to overcome the fact that police couldn't pin the electrically altered dice table on them. They pleaded guilty to a simple charge of gambling, and each paid a $150 fine and $8.81 in court costs.

And then came the big one. On June 2, 1953, Checkers went on trial before Federal Judge Willis W. Ritter, a bizarre figure in American jurisprudence, for failure to pay income taxes on $5,000 in 1946. Judge Ritter, who died in 1978, produced a series of strange judicial decisions during his twenty-nine years on the bench, including citing thirty postal workers for contempt of court because their mail-sorting machinery, located in the Post Office

Stylishly dressed, Clyde, *left*, and Checkers Smaldone stride out of the federal courthouse in 1953 after posting bond in a case that would send both to prison. © *The Denver Post*

Building that housed the federal court, was too noisy. An incredible 58 percent of his civil cases and 40 percent of his criminal cases were reversed.[1] Attorneys Zarlengo and Dickerson represented Checkers. Fast-rising US district attorney Charles Vigil was the prosecutor.

It was a contentious procedure from day one. Judge Ritter, whose fondness for Wild Turkey preceded him, was brought in from Salt Lake City to try the case. A hard-nosed, letter-of-the-law jurist, he wasn't happy when, on the first day of the trial in Denver, Dickerson asked that it be delayed because Checkers was ill. Denied, said Judge Ritter. At 9:30 AM the next day, all were assembled in Judge Ritter's courtroom, but Checkers failed to appear. Dickerson told the court that his client was at Mercy Hospital, "in pain." An irate Judge Ritter scolded Dickerson, "I thought I made it clear Monday that I wanted that man here for trial. You get him here." After a brief recess, during which Dickerson raced from the courtroom downtown to Mercy Hospital on the city's east side to fetch Checkers, the trial resumed, but not until Judge Ritter ordered Checkers's $10,000 property bond revoked for his failure to appear.

It turned out Checkers really was ill. During a court recess that afternoon, he was stricken with appendicitis and was rushed back to the hospital for surgery. When the trial resumed ten days later, Judge Ritter, angry that Checkers had taken his leave without telling the court, said from the bench, "That fellow acted in defiance of the United States of America as reposed in this court. I am not going to permit the defendant to play fast and loose with the United States court."[2] The maneuvering on both sides was for naught. Unable to come to a verdict, the jury was dismissed and a new trial set for September 1953. Checkers's attorneys asked that another judge be appointed to hear the case because, they said, Ritter was biased and prejudiced against the defendant. He refused to step down.

Amidst rumors of sensational findings by the ongoing federal grand jury, Checkers's second trial for tax evasion was postponed indefinitely. Based on testimony to the grand jury, Judge Ritter ordered the arrest of Checkers, Clyde, their cousin Louis Smaldone, uncle Fiore "Fat" Smaldone, and three other men, brothers Michael and Jerry Benallo Jr., and William "Willie" Calvaresi, on charges of conspiring to bribe jurors in Checkers's first tax-evasion trial. Judge Ritter called them "extremely serious charges."

On October 21, the brothers Smaldone surprised everyone, including their codefendants and the court, when they stood in front of Federal Judge W. Lee Knous, sitting in for Judge Ritter, who had gone back to Salt Lake City on vacation, and pleaded guilty to a single charge of conspiracy. They were nowhere near in the clear, however, because they and the five other defendants were about to go on trial for thirteen counts of jury tampering, to which all pleaded innocent

Judge Ritter was back in court when the jury-tampering trial began on October 28. A series of witnesses took the stand to describe how they were approached by men representing the Smaldones. Mrs. Effie Alsup, a neighbor of Calvaresi's in the small farm community of Dupont northeast of Denver, said Jerry Benallo Jr. promised that if she "sat down" on the jury (voted for acquittal), she would be rewarded with "a nice little gift."

"Did you feel he was offering you a bribe?" prosecutor Vigil asked.

"Why, sure I did."

Another woman said Fiore Smaldone asked her to "hang the jury." Four others told of being offered cash bribes ranging from $250 to $350 by friends and relatives of the Smaldones. Vigil called it "a brazen, thoroughly organized effort, with the planners armed with lists of prospective jurors," although how the accused men obtained the names was never brought out in court.[3] The prosecution paraded twenty-three witnesses to the stand. The Smaldones didn't testify in their own defense, but Dickerson told the court that his clients were only attempting to make sure they got a fair trial and that potential jurors would be "fair-minded."[4]

In his closing argument, Vigil told the jury of six men and six women that the Smaldone brothers "are snakes who are trying to destroy our system of jurisprudence." His assistant James Heyer backed him up. "The testimony you heard was as rotten as any testimony ever presented to any US jury in a federal courtroom."

After a fifty-minute explanation by Judge Ritter of the appropriate law, the jury got the case at 4:55 PM on Thursday, October 29, 1953, deliberated until 6:00, went to dinner until 8:00, deliberated some more, and announced at 9:45 that it had reached a verdict. Court clerk G. Walter Bowman read out the word *guilty* thirty-eight times. The courtroom clock stood at 9:55 PM The Smaldones' faces betrayed no emotion as the verdicts were read. Calvaresi buried his face in his hands. Frances, Checkers's wife, wept openly. Checkers, guilty of two conspiracy counts, eight counts of offering bribes to jurors, and eight counts of obstructing justice, calmly fired up one of his long cigars as he exited the courtroom in handcuffs. Clyde was found guilty of two counts of conspiracy and three counts each of offering bribes and obstructing justice. Five other men were guilty of identical, but fewer, counts. Judge Ritter—who, under the law, could sentence Checkers to 170 years and Clyde to 70 years and had said previously, "It is the court's opinion that murder and treason are no worse than attempting to bribe a jury"—ordered the seven defendants sent back to jail to await sentencing.

*The Post*, which had campaigned with horns and whistles against the Smaldone syndicate for more than three years, crowed in a headline, "Verdict Spells End of Smaldone Gang." The paper added in an editorial, "For too many years too many law-enforcement officers have had to devote too much of their time trying to bring a couple of small-time racketeers to justice. Most Denverites will hope we are through with the brothers Smaldone for some time to come…"[5]

Just how long became clear on November 23 when Judge Ritter sentenced each of the brothers to a whopping sixty years in federal prison and fined each man $24,000. If carried out, these were life sentences, because Clyde was forty-seven years old and Checkers was forty-three. William Calvaresi and Jerry Benallo Jr. each got fifteen years and a $5,000 fine, and Michael Benallo received ten years and a $5,000 fine. Charges against Louis Smaldone were dropped for lack of evidence, and Fiore Smaldone, whose health wasn't good, was sentenced to eighteen months at the US medical center in Springfield, Missouri. Judge Ritter gave defense attorneys five days to file appeals.

Attorney Dickerson announced that there would be an immediate appeal to the circuit court on behalf of the Smaldones. While awaiting transfer to the federal penitentiary in Leavenworth, Kansas, Clyde and Checkers spent Christmas 1953 in the Denver County Jail. There were no presents, no special privileges. They and the other inmates celebrated the holiday with fried chicken, cranberry sauce, celery dressing, and pumpkin pie. Their families were allowed to visit only between 1 and 3 PM. The Associated Press named the fall of the Smaldone empire 1953's number-one story in the state, beating out President Dwight D. Eisenhower's vacation in Colorado and the strangulation of a Denver telephone operator.

While all this was going on, the Smaldones were engaged in a desperate fight with city officials over the liquor license at Gaetano's, the restaurant centerpiece of the family's life. Melville launched an all-out war on the eatery when he declared in November 1951 that Gaetano's should be shut down because it was a hangout for hoodlums, the place where "schemes" of the gambling syndicate were hatched. Melville had proof that the Ace Cooperative, a front for the brothers' slot machine operations in Jefferson County, was headquartered at Gaetano's: the company's address was listed in the phone book as 3760 Tejon Street, the address of Gaetano's, a revelation that merited a large eight-column headline on the front page of The Post. At Melville's behest, the police department also began an investigation of his well-publicized charges that at least three of its officers were tipping the Smaldone mob to upcoming raids.

On paper, the restaurant and bar—and the liquor

It was headline news when the Smaldone brothers drew an astonishing sixty years each for jury tampering, but the sentences were shortened to twelve years on appeal. © Colorado Historical Society, *The Denver Post*, November 23, 1953

license—were owned by Mamie Smaldone, mother of Clyde and Checkers, a mythic arrangement made necessary because the brothers were felons and ineligible to hold a license. Melville wasn't buying it.

Melville and manager of safety Harold MacArthur launched what they called a citywide drive on questionable liquor licenses, but the real target was the Smaldones, because getting after the high-profile mobsters created buckets of publicity. Even the cops believed Gaetano's was being targeted. "There are plenty of places right downtown where they have served drunks and minors," one told *The Post*. "There hasn't been a single offense of that sort at Gaetano's, and nobody'd be fool enough to start a disturbance out there—not with the Smaldones around."[6] Later, National Football League officials were barred by the league from even entering the eatery.

William Blood, a former FBI man who succeeded MacArthur as Denver's manager of safety in 1952, kept up the pressure, requiring all liquor dealers and tavern owners to fill out a questionnaire that revealed their profits and to whom the money went. The newly formed Denver Beverage Dealers—led by Clyde Smaldone—declared Blood's questionnaire was "nosey and far too personal."

By December, the city dropped any pretense of a citywide crackdown and simply refused to renew Gaetano's liquor license for 1953. Its owners were given until December 31, 1952, to find a buyer. The family tried, first with nephew Paulie Villano, a bartender at the restaurant, who said he'd agreed to buy the place for $35,000, including a $10,000 cash loan from his father, Mike. Blood put up a serious roadblock. He would okay the sale, he said, if the

Smaldones would admit that they were the real owners, if Villano's father would sign an affidavit that he loaned his son the money, and if Villano would give Blood copies of his tax returns for the past two years.

Too many ifs. The deal didn't go through. At midnight on December 31, Gaetano's license expired, although the restaurant continued to operate without liquor. It was a disaster. Business virtually dried up. Without the license, the restaurant's value dropped from an estimated $100,000 to about half that. The restaurant limped along until December 1955, when Anthony Smaldone, a brother without a felony record, announced that he had purchased it from Mamie, Checkers and Clyde, and their wives, Frances and Mildred, and his brother Chauncey. He wanted the license back.

No deal, said new manager of safety Ed Geer. This time, the refusal was based on the discovery by an assistant city attorney that the area was zoned B-2, which prohibited the sale of intoxicants or 3.2 beer, although there were numerous other taverns in the neighborhood. Despite a large crowd of North Denver supporters and the plea of Anthony's attorney Richard Shaw that Gaetano's was "one of the cleanest and finest restaurants in Denver,"[7] Geer turned aside the request.

Anthony sued Geer and the city, claiming that Geer's denial was "illegal, arbitrary and capricious, without good cause, contrary to the overwhelming wishes and needs of the inhabitants within the area and a gross abuse of [Geer's] discretion as the licensing authority."[8] District court judge Edward Keating overruled Geer's decision, and Anthony got his license.

Vigil had managed the jury-tampering case against the Smaldones brilliantly but had little time to bask in the warmth of his victory. In the midst of chasing the case against the brothers, Vigil, appointed by Truman, a Democrat, was fired in 1953 via press release by US attorney general Herbert Brownell at the direction of President Dwight D. Eisenhower, a Republican. Brownell appointed a college fraternity brother to replace Vigil, who got the news through a phone call from a reporter. It was partisan politics at its seamiest. Truman called it "born of intention or stupidity." Vigil was allowed to stay on as special prosecutor until the Smaldones were convicted, an outcome embarrassing to administration officials, who tried to paint Vigil as unfit to hold his office. In a lengthy tribute to him, *The Post* wrote, "Behind him he will leave a trail of jailed gangsters—topped by the Smaldone mob—and imprisoned income-tax evaders, narcotics dealers, mail-thief rings, community credit violators, hoodlums, and gamblers."[9]

After his dismissal, Vigil, who died in 1999 at age eighty-six, went into private practice in Denver and Trinidad, ran unsuccessfully for state attorney general against Duke Dunbar in 1954, and regained some measure of publicity in 1955 when he was named one of three defense lawyers for John Gilbert Graham, executed for blowing up his mother and forty-three others on a United Airlines flight.

Melville spent the majority of his public career as assistant district attorney in Denver and died in 1959 at age sixty-seven while a partner in a law firm with Fred Winner and William Berge. *The Post* said of him in an editorial, "Among those who will miss him most are the newspapermen for whom he was a friend and a legal consultant (unpaid)."[10]

Their guilty verdicts meant Clyde and Checkers were headed to Leavenworth as guests of the federal government. As they waited in the marshal's office in the courthouse to be returned to the county jail after they were found guilty, their lead attorney, Fred Dickerson, tried to cheer them up. "Don't give up hope. We're in there fighting for you."[11]

Federal Judge Willis W. Ritter, whose bizarre rulings were frequently overturned, was ordered by the US Supreme Court to be replaced for the Smaldones' second jury-tampering trial in 1955. © *The Denver Post*

# CHAPTER THIRTEEN

# DOUBLE-CROSSED

*[Judge] Knous says he was going to give us twelve years—four, four, and four, and run 'em concurrently. Instead of that, he run 'em consecutively, so we had twelve years. Yeah. I don't think that was fair for that much time.*

—Clyde Smaldone

The heat was smothering. As the brothers Smaldone and their two US marshal escorts rolled along Highway 40 across the baked plains of eastern Colorado and the endless horizons of Kansas in an unair-conditioned automobile, they passed through a string of oases, farm communities really. Burlington, Colby, Russell, Junction City slid past slowly on the 600-mile road trip to their new home; the United States Penitentiary at Leavenworth, Kansas, just up the Missouri River from Kansas City.

To Clyde and Checkers Smaldone, it felt like the last time they would see Colorado.

After the US Supreme Court agreed in March 1955 with their attorneys that the sentences handed them by Judge Willis W. Ritter were capricious and excessive, the Smaldones and their cohorts in the jury-tampering trial got a second chance. The high court took only thirty-seven words to grant the defendants a second trial: "*Per Curiam:* In the interest of justice and in the exercise of the supervisory powers of this court, *certiorari* is granted and cases are severally reversed and remanded to the district court for retrial before a different judge."

Buried in the turgid legalese was the key phrase "before a different judge." It pointedly took the case out of the hands of the mercurial Judge Ritter, whose aggressive attitude toward the Smaldones and their associates—at one point he gave Clyde 370 years before cutting it to 170, then 60 years—was obvious. Even *The Denver Post*, which campaigned loudly against the crime syndicate in its columns, approved of the decision. In an editorial, it took on those who claimed the new trial smacked of "leniency." Rather, said the paper, "The Supreme Court was merely protecting the impartiality of our legal procedures, without which none of us could survive for long."[1]

Their previous convictions tossed, Checkers pleaded guilty to jury tampering in June 1955, and Clyde's trial—twice delayed because, said his lawyers, he was suffering from "severe anxiety reaction"—began on July 10, 1955, in front of Federal Judge W. Lee Knous. The judge was a native Coloradan and onetime mayor of Montrose, Colorado, state senator, and Colorado Supreme Court justice who had served as governor from 1947 to 1950, a job he resigned when he was appointed to the US District Court for Colorado. He was regarded as an even-handed jurist whose lone bit of flair was an ever-present bow tie.

The trial wasn't two days old when Clyde Smaldone, like his brother, pleaded guilty to three counts involving tampering: general conspiracy to fix a jury and two counts of attempt to obstruct justice. In exchange, the government dropped nineteen other charges, including 1953 slot

Clyde and Checkers Smaldone felt double-crossed by Judge W. Lee Knous, who gave them three consecutive four-year terms after they pleaded guilty in exchange for concurrent sentences. © *The Denver Post*

machine violations and obstruction of justice, out of which Checkers's tax-evasion trial had sprung.

All that remained was for Judge Knous to sentence the Smaldones and four others. Fred Dickerson, the Smaldones' attorney, pleaded that both men contributed heavily to their church and already had been given severe penalties. Judge Knous responded, "These men started out deliberately with a well-organized plan...to corrupt a jury. That overshadowed in my mind the good things they have done."[2] The *Rocky Mountain News* said that Judge Knous was at a loss to understand how anyone could "deliberately attempt to corrupt the most sacred part of our judicial system."[3]

On August 19, before a courtroom filled with defendants, lawyers, family members, and spectators, Judge Knous sentenced both Clyde and Checkers to twelve years at Leavenworth, and each was fined $10,000. The judgment and commitment order on Criminal Case 13833, signed by Judge Knous, read, "It is adjudged that the defendant is hereby committed to the custody of the Attorney General or his authorized representative for imprisonment for a period of four (4) years on Count 1 of the Indictment herein, said term of imprisonment to run consecutively with the terms of imprisonment imposed in Criminal Case No. 13776 and Criminal Case No. 13794. It is further ordered by the Court that Count 2 of the Indictment herein be and the same hereby dismissed."[4]

As their sentences were read, the brothers, wrote reporter Bob Pattridge in *The Post*, "stood calm with their hands behind their backs and Judge Knous told them that they obstructed 'the most sacred thing in our judicial system,' the jury panel."[5] He might have given them fifteen years apiece, but, he said, he took into account that both men had already served fourteen months at Leavenworth and another six months in the Denver County Jail awaiting trial on their previous convictions.

The other defendants, all of whom pleaded not guilty but were convicted anyway, were given lesser sentences. Checkers's brother-in-law, Joseph Cefalu, who became the eighth defendant in the case after the first trial, received two and a half years and a $5,000 fine for obstructing justice; Fiore Smaldone got eighteen months and a $5,000 fine for obstructing justice; and William Calvaresi and Jerry Benallo Jr. each were sentenced to eighteen months and fines of $3,000 and $500, respectively, for offering a bribe. Michael Benallo's conviction on one count of conspiracy was reversed by the US Circuit Court of Appeals.

The defendants appeared calm inside the courtroom, but they were anything but when they got outside the Post Office Building in Denver that housed the federal courts.

The Smaldones' cousin, Fiore, a squat, pear-shaped man also known as Fat, called the gathered newspapermen "sons of bitches from Arkansas," although no one was sure what that meant. Clyde stood silent, grim-faced, and Checkers tried to punch a photographer. Dickerson told reporters, "These men were tried by the newspapers, television and by radio. It doesn't excuse the offense but it does indicate something in the country that has to be arrested."[6]

To the public, it appeared cut and dried—the Smaldones pleaded and the government gave them a deal—but the brothers were adamant that they had been double-crossed, an unpardonable sin in their world, where a man's word was his bond. "[Judge] Knous says he was going to give

A 1982 photograph seems to show Checkers Smaldone knocking down *Rocky Mountain News* photographer Linda McConnell, but she later said that she fell backward and he inadvertently ran into her. © *The Denver Post*

us twelve years—four, four, and four, and run 'em concurrently," Clyde recalled in 1992. "Instead of that, he run 'em consecutively, so we had twelve years. Yeah. I don't think that was fair for that much time. But, I guess that's the way they do it. The papers crucified us." Once they pleaded guilty, there was no taking it back. They were stuck. "I went to jail for my brother for nine and a half years and then he didn't even pay my fine, a $10,000 fine! He shoulda paid it, he ain't paid me to this day!" Clyde never forgave Checkers for dragging him into it, a breach that contributed to the two men drifting apart in later years.

Had Judge Knous lived up to his part of the bargain the Smaldones thought they had made, they would have received four years, gotten time off for the twenty months they already had been locked up, and probably would have been released in two years. Instead, they were saddled with ten years behind bars.

In 1956, the family considered appealing the sentences a second time. From his cell in Leavenworth, Clyde wrote a letter to the clerk of the District Court requesting the costs of obtaining copies of various court documents, "all material related to my action taken in our second hearing and trial and guilty pleas too."[7] The prestigious Washington, DC, law firm of Ford and Larson, which carried the first, successful Smaldone appeal to the US Supreme Court, looked into it. Noted attorney Peyton Ford, later assistant attorney general in the Nixon administration, wrote to Checkers's wife, Frances, and Clyde's wife, Mildred, advising them to think it over carefully. In a nineteen-page memorandum, Ford explained pertinent parts of the law and the validity of the indictments against the brothers.

As may be seen from this memorandum, the issues involved are extremely complex and not susceptible to a quick or easy decision. Furthermore, at least with respect to some of the issues, they suggest a revolving door: By raising one, we may lose another; by taking one position, we may destroy another position. Accordingly, it would appear that the discussion contained in this memorandum be carefully considered by all concerned. Moreover, since this case has already once been before the Supreme Court, it may be that the Supreme Court feels some sort of pro-prietary interest in the proceedings, and would not feel that the District Court and the Court of Appeals were important prerequisites.[8]

In short, the Supreme Court was unlikely to look kindly on a decision they'd already made being brought back to them. This, and the potential time and cost involved in starting the process over—they'd already spent thousands of dollars on lawyers—convinced the family to pass up another appeal.

The entire episode might have been avoided if Checkers had stepped up, swallowed, however hard, and paid the federal taxes he owed. He wouldn't do it. Clyde said, "I begged him to go and pay his taxes and he says, 'Well, they beat me out of $40,000, and when I won the $40,000 back the government stepped in and said, "Where'd you get this money?" And that's why they filed on it.' And so we tried to help him, but I didn't talk to no jurors but I got sentenced because I talked to people that might know somebody who [sat] on the jury. I done nine and a half years for that. I felt I shouldn't have got that kinda time and, anyhow, the deal was, anytime there's a Smaldone or any friends got in trouble, they always give 'em maximum time. Everybody else, they give 'em a medal, I think. Not that I give a damn, but I don't like to see nobody go to jail, but be fair to everybody."

When the Smaldones left Denver at 6 AM on Sunday, August 21, 1955, for the drive across the Great Plains to Leavenworth, with them were two deputy US marshals and a third prisoner, Robert Day, headed to the pen for a year for transporting a firearm in interstate commerce. When they arrived, they, like all prisoners, went through quarantine, were photographed, and were issued dark blue prison clothes.

The prison looked like a prison should. Leavenworth was known as "the hot house," and not fondly. A lack of air-conditioning made the hot and humid Kansas summers intolerable. It's also known as The Big Top for the rotunda built in 1926 at the front gate. Forty-foot-high walls (which penetrate forty feet below ground to discourage burrowers) sit on 1,583 acres, with 22.8 acres inside the walls. It opened in 1903 when the first 418 inmates, previously housed at the military prison at Fort Leavenworth three miles away, moved in.

Clyde's organizational skills came in handy at Leavenworth. The prison was a mess. Corruption was pervasive until new chief culinary steward, George W. Stouder, arrived. "He knew that they was stealing all the money and we were starving. They was going to have a big riot. Stouder called me up in the office one day. He says, 'Why don't you come up here and we'll work out something so we can get this place straightened out?' So we start to fixing up because, boy, that place was terrible. We used to get cold oatmeal in the morning. Real rotten milk. Black coffee, terrible. They had us sitting in the dining room on benches.

"When we got through fixing that place up, there was no more machine guns up on the walk. We got tables and chairs in the dining room. It took us three years to fix it. When we left prison, the place was like an angel's place, new tables and chairs, and we cleaned out the cockroaches and mice and the rats out of the cellblocks. It was terrible, terrible, filthy, dirty."

While they were "reforming" the prison, the Smaldones also worked in the kitchen. "There was twenty of us in there. Everything was clean and we made good food. With the help of other inmates, we fed 8,000 meals a day." Some credited the boys with introducing pizza to the prison menu. Clyde, in fact, was awarded a certificate in culinary sanitation and another for learning baking. In an accompanying letter, W. M. Arnold, director of the state board for vocational education, wrote to Clyde, "You have proved to us that you have the ability and courage that are necessary to do a job in the trade for which you have prepared yourself."[9] In addition, he took up painting and demonstrated some abilities—except for rendering hands, which he got a fellow prisoner/artist to teach him.

Checkers, who never went to school past the eighth grade, grew interested in education too. He told a friend in Denver during one of his court appearances that while he was at Leavenworth he was taking college-level classes in psychology and anthropology.

They also rubbed elbows with some of the prison's "celebrities." "I was in with [New York mobster] Vito Genovese," Clyde said. "He was a nice guy too. Machine Gun Kelly, he was a nobody, a big fake." Dallas gambler Benny Binion, who later owned the famed Horseshoe Casino in Las Vegas, was there. "My brother and I saved his life. He was under constant watch by the guards. He'd wait for us, and we'd walk around in the yard. Nobody bothered him."

Clyde became a favorite of management. "All the white-collar workers in the Leavensworth prison, they all liked me. Mr. [James] Bennett, the head of all the prisons in the United States, he never did go see a man without a guard or anything. Mr. Stouder and him was waiting for me when they called for me and we had a long talk. He thanked me and said, 'You did a lot of good for the prison.' Which I did."

Not everyone was so taken with Clyde. One guard was resentful of his closeness to the administration because it was Clyde who carried orders from Stouder to the culinary staff. "One of the [guards] that worked in the culinary department, he come to me about five days before I was going to get out, called me on the side. He says, 'Smaldone, we're gonna frame you, we're gonna get you. There's five of us gonna frame you, and you're not gonna go home in five days.' I looked at him and I says, 'Listen…and I grabbed him by the arm—and that's twenty years alone—and I said, 'Let's go in to the associated warden, and I want you to tell him what you're telling me.' Well, the goof backed down, and I never told nobody anything about it, but there was convicts there that heard the whole argument.

"So, the next morning, Stouder comes. [He said], 'Oh, you don't have to come to the [culinary] department. Why don't you rest? You've only got a few days.' I didn't tell Stouder about this until he retired and he came to see me in Denver once. He says, 'No, I know you didn't tell me, but three or four people come in and told me. We had a trap set for them. There'd been five guards [who] lost their jobs.'"

The Smaldones were kept under protective custody during their last days at Leavenworth. Stouder and his assistant, Joe Fontana, even drove them to Kansas City after their release to board the plane for Denver. "I wanted to buy both of them a present, [but] I was so happy about it I forgot about it," Clyde recalled.

Having served a little more than seven years during their second trip to Leavenworth, Clyde and Checkers returned home in November 1962. They were turned down for parole three times during their stay at Leavenworth. Some, especially the brothers, saw the hand of Bobby Kennedy, the president's brother, the man in charge of the Justice Department and an ardent crime fighter, behind the refusals. While they were locked up, *Gunsmoke* made its television debut, Joe DiMaggio was elected to the Baseball Hall of Fame, the Soviet Union launched *Sputnik*, Alaska and Hawaii became states, the Air Force Academy opened, John Glenn became the first American to orbit the Earth, and death took Arturo Toscanini, Marilyn Monroe, James Dean, Ty Cobb, and Eleanor Roosevelt.

Another important event took place. Their beloved mother, Mamie, died of cancer the previous May at the age of seventy-two. A tireless church worker, she was a woman, said her daughter Angie Capra, "who never turned a beggar away from her door." When she was taken terminally ill seven months earlier, prison officials gave the Smaldones the option of visiting her then or attending her funeral. They chose to see her while she was alive. "I hope you will be kind," Angie told *The Post*. "She was a wonderful mother to all of us."[10]

Still camera shy and disdainful of newspapermen, the boys eluded publicity when they arrived at Stapleton Field in Denver on a snowy November day. "They [the media] was waiting with cameras at the airfield. We had 'em fooled. A friend of ours opened one gate where we could go through and they wouldn't get a shot at us. Then we came home and we were home, thank God."

Clyde, fifty-six, who loathed the media, nevertheless sat down with *The Post* for a long homecoming interview a few days later. He was conciliatory and, of course, charming. "I've got no animosity against anyone. It's all over now. Let's forget the past. We're going to try to make a living and make it legitimately." He harbored only one grudge—that Flip-Flop nickname. "I never had that nickname. I don't know where [the newspapers] got it. I wouldn't have minded if it was my nickname. But it wasn't."[11]

Now that he was back home, the first order of business was to try to mend fences within the family.

Chauncey Smaldone, *left*, and his nephew Paulie Villano took over control of the family's enterprises in the 1960s while Clyde and Checkers were serving time. © *The Denver Post*

# CHAPTER FOURTEEN

# CHAUNCEY, PAULIE, AND EUGENE

*Things...work better for you...if you are who you are.*

—Ronnie Bay, describing Paulie Villano

With their departure for the federal penitentiary at Leavenworth, Kansas, for a probable ten-year stretch in 1955, Clyde and Checkers Smaldone had left the family businesses—Gaetano's restaurant, loans, and gambling—in the hands of their youngest brother, Clarence, better known as Chauncey, and their nephew Paulie Villano.

Clarence Michael "Chauncey" Smaldone was the youngest of the eleven children born to Raffaele and Mamie Smaldone. Born in Denver on February 8, 1924, he was the couple's sixth son, almost two decades younger than his eldest brother, Clyde. As a child, he roamed the North Denver neighborhood with his nephew Paulie, only four years younger, and the two became inseparable. Villano and his family lived at 3048 West Forty-first Avenue, next door to Clyde Smaldone and his family at 3042.

Chauncey was dead-on the best looking of the brothers, and much taller than the others, almost six feet. Blessed with a full head of wavy hair, which he never lost, and piercing dark eyes, he bore a striking resemblance as a young man to crooner Dean Martin.

This did not go unnoticed by young ladies in his largely Italian neighborhood. "I thought he was nice looking," said

Pauline Blasi Smaldone, who met Chauncey as a teenager and married him when both were nineteen years old. "I had a girlfriend that lived off of Thirty-sixth Avenue. She used to live down there and I'd go down and see her, and Chauncey, he was standing in front of Canino's Pool Hall, Thirty-sixth and Navajo. I didn't know who he was. She told me." Later, Pauline and another school friend, Babe, were riding the streetcar into downtown Denver when she said, "'Babe, look, that car, it looks like it's following the streetcar.' She said, 'Oh, that's Chauncey Smaldone.' And we get downtown and we went around a little bit and then he parked his car somewhere, and he was following us. Then he asked if he could take us home. I told Babe, 'I don't know if I want to go with him. I don't even know him.'" They took the streetcar home.

"I kept seeing him around the pool hall all the time, and one day she introduced me to him. It was right after I got out of [high] school. I got out of school in June, and it was in July when I met him, and we started going together right away."[1]

As it did for a lot of couples, World War II interrupted their courtship. In 1942, Chauncey enlisted in the army, which promptly shipped him off to San Antonio, Texas, for basic training. In Texas barely two months, he wrote to Pauline to tell her that he wanted to marry her. "We were going to wait until he come out of the service, but it didn't work that way. I bought the dress and my dad took me, we all drove down [to Texas]. We got married August 1, 1943."[2]

It was not an easy beginning. "I never got a honeymoon. We just stayed [in military housing]. It was miserable hot. I think it was 120 in the shade. Oh, it was awful. We stayed there three months, and then they moved him. I come home and they moved Chauncey to California. When he settled there, me, my mother-in-law, [and] my brother-in-law Ralph went down to Los Angeles to be with Chauncey. Then they shipped him out. Then I come home and I had my son [in September 1944]. He didn't see Paul until he was about sixteen months old."[3] Chauncey returned to Denver from the South Pacific at war's end and they had a second child, Claudia Jean, whom they called C. J., born in 1949.

Like many young couples, when the war ended they settled into family life. Chauncey moved his wife and son into an apartment above Gaetano's restaurant and began working in a filling station he and Villano operated at West Forty-sixth Avenue and Pecos Street. Neither man was particularly adept mechanically, but in addition to pumping gas, they were running gambling in a back room. Pauline helped out the family budget by cooking and waitressing at the restaurant, a job she kept for fifteen years. Chauncey also sometimes worked behind the bar at Gaetano's. Nephew Paulie Villano eventually found his niche running the restaurant.

Paul Clyde Villano was called Fat Paulie by those who knew him and by a lot of those who didn't. It was a nickname that stuck with him and, at the same time, irritated him, even though a special on Gaetano's menu was Fat Paulie's Terrorizer Pizza. Villano was born January 1, 1928, the only son of eldest Smaldone sister, Corinne, whom he lived with and cared for until her death in 1991. Friends recalled him as a terrific tap dancer as a youth,

Chauncey, *left*, the youngest Smaldone brother, ran the bar at the family's thriving Gaetano's restaurant in North Denver in the fifties and sixties while his brothers were in prison. The other bartender is Jenary Pisicchio. © Smaldone Family Collection

a champion gymnast in high school, and a scholarship athlete at the University of Colorado, but in later years he "filled out," earning the Fat Paulie sobriquet.

Villano, who never married, was a devout ladies' man. When he had money, which was often, he spent freely on alcohol and beautiful women and made frequent trips to Las Vegas to partake of both. "He had more flight attendants," recalled Shirley Smaldone, wife of Anthony, another of the Smaldone brothers, who also worked at Gaetano's. "He would bring them into the restaurant, once a month, and he would introduce me, or whoever was around there, and they were all beautiful gals, and when he came back, I says, 'How do you get all these good-looking girls?' 'Because I'm such a good guy, and I'm a good-looker.' To me, he wasn't."[4]

"You know, Paulie wasn't an ugly duckling," said Ronnie Bay, who knew him since boyhood. "He was a good-looking kid, and he was looking pretty good, at that point. He wasn't out of shape and all. You know, you got a few bucks and you're not bashful about buying a beer because you can afford two or three of them, things like that work better for you...if you are who you are, and you're meeting Chauncey and you're meeting Clyde or whoever, it's sort of like 'Whoa!,' you know?"[5]

Like his Uncle Clyde, Paulie was charming and an adept storyteller. Also like his uncle, he loved pranks, sometimes putting on a tough-guy telephone voice and frightening people. Until he quit drinking, he could command a barroom setting—he always stood, never sat at the bar—but when he'd had too much, he would become loud and friends would avoid him.

He was a social animal. He always seemed to be in motion, frequently telling companions, "I gotta go meet a guy." His reputation as an erratic driver didn't stop him from frequently touring his bookmaking accounts and visiting friends. Al Ursetta, who owned a construction company and played barbooth in Smaldone-run games on East Colfax Avenue and on Federal Boulevard, recalled, "He was really a character. He came to the office almost every day of the week and would bring donuts. Years ago, he could be mean. He was a big man."[6]

It wasn't long before Chauncey and Paulie joined Clyde and Checkers in the family enterprises: gambling and sports parlay cards. And it wasn't long after that, in 1956, that Chauncey, thirty-two, rang up his first gambling arrest when he and seven others were busted at a house at 3357 Navajo Street and charged with running a barbooth game, an old family favorite.

At that point, the Smaldones' political connections came into play. Councilman Sonny Mapelli, who represented North Denver, invoked a little-known provision in the city ordinances that allowed councilmen to order released from jail accused violators without bond or approval of judges. Mapelli told the papers that he "knew the whole Smaldone family" and considered Chauncey a friend. In the end, Smaldone and all but one of those arrested went to trial but were set free by a judge because, he said, police failed to prove that the men were actually caught gambling.

Chauncey rang up a series of arrests—and a lot of acquittals—for gambling in the 1960s and 1970s. There were a couple of sentences for several months in prison and some fines. The Smaldone outfit, however, was moving out of dice gaming and into loan-sharking and parlay betting cards, low-percentage gambling for those on a budget. Players could get in for a buck or two and pick several baseball, college basketball, or football games. Point spreads, not the final score, determined winners and losers. But Chauncey and Paulie weren't in with just the small-time gamblers; high-stakes bettors booked with them as well.

Paulie's reputation as a bookmaker was flawless. He collected on time when he won, paid out immediately when he didn't. Onetime rock music promoter Barry Fey placed bets with Paulie for more than two years. "He always paid; he was always on time," remembered Fey. "There was never, 'You said this, he said this.' He always got information right. He was a very nice guy, not the prototypical mob guy as the newspapers and others would have him made out." Fey recalled a moment in 1971:

> It was the year when Oklahoma, Nebraska, and Colorado, they all went to bowl games and they were all favored and they all just crushed their opposition. And I bet, I think it was $10,000 on each and a $5,000 parlay, so that means he had to pay me $55,000. One of the times that I won a lot he comes to the office to pay and there's another guy with him. And the guy sticks out his hand and says, "Hi, I'm Chauncey Smaldone." I said, "Hi, how are you?" He says, "I just wanted to make sure that there was a human being involved in this. I've never seen a guy beat Paulie so bad so consistently." Paulie didn't say nothing. He just stood there.[7]

Paul "Fat Paulie" Villano had an unsullied reputation as a bookmaker who paid off when he lost and collected promptly when he won. He died in 2003. © *The Denver Post*

Villano and Fey became good friends, based on mutual need. "A couple of times I was short of cash, he was always there," Fey said. "I said, 'Paulie, I need five, I need three.' He sometimes came to the office to drop it off because he loved getting [concert] tickets. He brought candy all the time for [Fey's assistant] Mel Gibson and everybody. I mean, anytime there was a big show, you knew Paulie was going to be calling for tickets, and we would try to accommodate him when we could, and he would always pay; he never asked for anything for free."

Villano found his niche overseeing the restaurant at Gaetano's. "Nobody could run Gaetano's like Paulie," said his barber, friend, and fellow bookmaker Jerry Middleton. "Oh, my God, he threw some parties there. And the food! Whatever was the best—provolone, sausage—wasn't good enough for Paulie. Then, all of a sudden, Paulie and Chauncey got into a beef. Paulie owned the parking lot across the street. He was going to put a fence around it, and then Gaetano's wouldn't have any parking. He never did it."[8]

His reputation as a fun-loving guy aside, Paulie was smart and college-educated. "If you were in a conversation with Paulie, or if he'd read something in the newspaper that was wrong, he'd go ballistic," said another bookmaker. In his working relationship with Chauncey, it was Paulie who had the greater smarts. And he had taste. He insisted that the Subway Tavern & Pizzeria, just down Thirty-eighth Avenue from Gaetano's, where he went frequently for pizza, carry a certain brand of olive oil, just for his use.

With Checkers and Clyde gone, Chauncey and Paulie ran the operation and it was understood that they were in charge. But their management skills (and the muscle to back them up) were short of the older brothers. The situation with nephew Eugene Smaldone was just one example of where their muscle fell short.

Independent of Chauncey and Paulie, and probably without their knowledge, Young Eugene, Checkers's son, was dipping into the bookmaking and loan-sharking operations. Riding his father's reputation for toughness, he collected thousands of dollars from local gamblers and those who had loans outstanding, but the monies never made it to the syndicate's coffers. When the Smaldone brothers came home from prison and tried to collect what they thought were outstanding debts, they were told, "We paid Eugene." He denied it.

In addition, Young Eugene was using and dealing narcotics, an anathema to the family, which was involved in numerous illegal activities, but drugs weren't among them. "I hate drugs and hate anybody'd fool with 'em or takes 'em. Anybody fools with dope is the filthiest scum on earth," Chauncey told *The Post*.[9]

Checkers declined for a long time to acknowledge his son's involvement with drugs, despite repeated warnings from those closest to him. Clyde once told him, half jokingly, "Why don't you just shoot him?" He was frequently in trouble with the law. Beginning in 1960, he was arrested, and sometimes convicted, on various charges, including bookmaking, burglary, gambling, conspiracy, racketeering,

Brothers Chauncey, *left*, and Checkers Smaldone were sentenced to ten years in 1982 for loan-sharking, income-tax evasion, and firearms violations. Chauncey, fifty-eight, and Checkers, seventy-two, were in the twilight of their careers. © *The Denver Post*

brawling, and drunk driving, all relatively minor, but in 1972 he received a ten-year sentence for importing cocaine from Peru after federal agents nabbed him with six pounds of the drug in his possession.

Young Eugene enjoyed the high life and spent money like he had it. His favorite vices were cocaine, heroin, luxury automobiles, high-roller trips to casinos in Las Vegas, and a strikingly beautiful blonde named Judy Good. His relationship with Good was tumultuous, and its consequences disastrous. Young Eugene, it turned out, wasn't the only Smaldone whose taste in women caused the family harm.

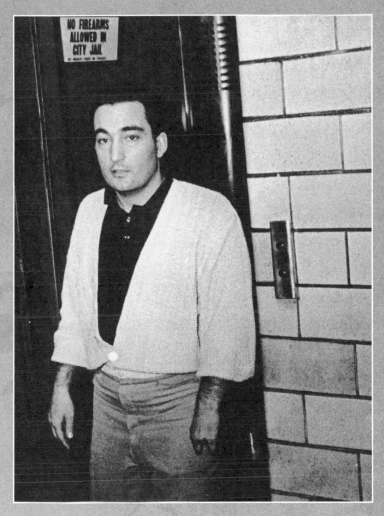

Young Eugene Smaldone, Checkers's son, became an anathema to the family because of his frequent drug dealing. In 1972, he got ten years for smuggling cocaine. © *The Denver Post*

Pauline Smaldone, who married Chauncey out of high school and helped run the family's bookmaking operations, was wounded in her front yard by two bullets. © *The Denver Post*

CHAPTER FIFTEEN

# THE SMALDONE WOMEN

*I'm not in the business, but if I was going to drop the hammer*
*on somebody, it would be her.*
—Friend of the Smaldone family speaking
about Jeannie Reeb Smaldone

Every family has its dysfunctional moments. In an Italian family it's akin to an opera: the stage is grander, the characters bigger than life. When the close-knit Smaldone clan came unraveled, it did so with fireworks and bombast, often at the hands of its female members.

Everyone thought Chauncey Smaldone was a one-woman man. After all, he had married his teenage sweetheart. "Pauline was the only woman he was ever with," remembered one family member. The only one, that is, until he crossed paths with Carol Jean "Jeannie" Reeb. They met in the 1970s when Jeannie set her sights on Chauncey and wouldn't turn him loose, despite the fact that he had spent thirty-five years married to Pauline.

What attracted Chauncey to Jeannie remains a mystery among the Smaldones, although one theorized that Pauline and Jeannie were both strong-willed women, the type Chauncey needed to get him motivated. Jeannie wasn't exactly "a catch." She had a police record dating to the mid-1950s that included numerous arrests and several convictions for petty theft and shoplifting. A confirmed

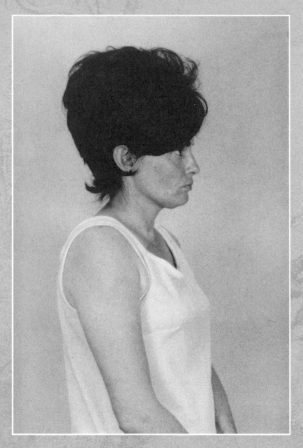

Chauncey's second wife, Jeannie Reeb Smaldone, was a convicted shoplifter who drew the wrath of the Smaldone family for breaking up his marriage and for taking control of Gaetano's restaurant. © Denver Police Department

kleptomaniac, she couldn't keep her hands off other people's stuff. "She'd go to somebody's house, somebody she knows, and pick this up and steal it, and she doesn't know why or care," Clyde's son Gene recalled.[1] At one point, she was arrested in Aspen for shoplifting a $300 Gucci leather purse and a silver-studded belt. In her defense, her lawyer argued that the charge should be lessened to a misdemeanor because the items were overpriced. The case was dropped because, said the district attorney, police searched her car improperly. Less than a year later, she was caught shoplifting again, this time over trivialities like $51 worth of meat and a package of Gummi Bears candy.

No Smaldone could think of a kind word to say about her. One friend of the family said, "I'm not in the business, but if I was going to drop the hammer on somebody, it would be her. She hurt a lot of people."

"I would spit on that girl," said Shirley Smaldone in 2007, then seventy-seven years old and a small woman whose eyes smoldered when she talked about Jeannie. "Oh, she was terrible! [Chauncey] was one guy who could get any girl he wanted, and he didn't want Pauline anymore. He wanted Jeannie, which was the worst mistake that man ever made in his life. That was it.

"She was on his back all the time. She wouldn't let him out of her sight. What the hell she did to that man, I don't know. She got what she wanted. She was happy she had him. Money, money, money. Whatever she wanted, she got."[2] In her heart, she wanted to be a Smaldone.

After Jeannie married Chauncey in 1982 and became more involved in the day-to-day operation of Gaetano's, the restaurant's food and business worsened, despite the best efforts of Clyde, Chauncey, and Paulie. She was a destructive force, right from the start. As she got more control of Chauncey, she gained more control over Gaetano's, and became a wedge between Chauncey and Paulie, who had been very close since childhood. She also nearly forced Shirley into bankruptcy, giving the Smaldone sister good reason to loathe Jeannie.

Jeannie regarded the place as her personal bank account. When anything went wrong or money was missing, she told Chauncey it was Paulie's fault. "She was pocketing all the money that came in. There was nothing in the bank," said Shirley. Chauncey took Jeannie's side, leading Paulie eventually to pull out of the business, which he had run very well given the circumstances, and the two men's friendship was irrevocably shattered.

Eventually, Jeannie became a part owner in the business, and that's when all hell broke loose. When Gaetano's opened in 1947, it was owned jointly by Clyde and his mother, Mamie, who insisted that her half of the building's ownership go to another son, Ralph, when she died. Eventually, Clyde's son Gene got his father's half when he died and Ralph was coerced to sign over his half to Chauncey and Jeannie, who split their share. When Chauncey later was taken ill, Jeannie took control of his 25 percent too.

Gaetano's liquor license, once held by soft-spoken brother Anthony Smaldone, never involved in the family's criminal activities, fell to his wife, Shirley, when he died. Shirley and Jeannie, both married to Smaldone brothers and both working at the restaurant, soon became fast friends, so it was no surprise when Jeannie asked Shirley to take out a $65,000 loan on her house to help support the business.

Jeannie was supposed to make the payments on the loan, but after a while, she quit. Nobody ever saw what became of the $65,000. "She just turned on me," said Shirley. "She maxed out all my credit cards, she didn't pay the house payments." Jeannie assured her that everything was okay. "The payment is in the mail" was her standard reply to Shirley's concerns.

One day, Gene Smaldone received a frantic call from the restaurant. "Two guys come into Gaetano's and said, 'We're going to take over management of Gaetano's.' These guys [had] read Shirley was in foreclosure, and they sweet-talked her and got her to sign over the title to her house and Gaetano's, management of Gaetano's."[3] Gene stepped in, convinced the two men that legal action would follow if they didn't turn over the documents to him and call off the deal. "If it hadn't been for Gene, I would be out on the street," said Shirley, who today lives in an apartment owned by Gene Smaldone.

Eventually the restaurant and building were sold to a restaurant company. Jeannie got paid for her share of the building but not the business. Said Gene, "When we sold the business, I made sure Shirley got Jeannie's share."[4] In October 2007, news reached the Smaldones that Jeannie had died in Mexico. No tears were shed by the family.

Pauline Smaldone was a family favorite. Bright, funny, and conversant, she fit in. While Clyde and Checkers were incarcerated, Pauline helped keep the family's bookmaking operations up and running by taking bets for Chauncey and Paulie.

In an interview in 2007, she explained how the system worked. "They have my number. I didn't even know the guys that were on the phones. I never saw 'em or anything. They didn't even use their right names. They didn't know who I was either. They would call me. Somebody calls [the bookmaker], he takes the bet, he calls me and gives me the bet. I keep all the bets."[5] This system put two steps between the players and the book, in case law enforcement stepped in.

Players were known by a code name or number, which could lead to humorous situations. Once, Paulie and Chauncey were at a hotel health spa on a pleasure trip to Las Vegas when Paulie said, "Look, there's 007!" "We don't have an 007," Chauncey said. "No, no. I mean James Bond in the movies," said Paulie, pointing out Sean Connery.

Pauline and Clyde's wife, Mildred, once ferried a large amount of cash from Denver to Omaha, Nebraska, to "lay off" bets. "We went to Omaha. We flew down. They would tell me the guy's name or explain what he would look like. I didn't know 'em. This guy come up. My God, he was so heavy! I forgot what name they even told me to ask for, and it was him. We just met in the airport." She didn't even know how much money they were carrying, but it was a lot, so much that the two women split it between their bulging purses. "That was the only time I had ever done that."[6]

Despite the fact that she was only marginally involved, Pauline was targeted in a shooting, even though family members were considered off-limits to violence. In the late afternoon of July 5, 1973, she walked to the front gate of her Lakewood house to get that day's *Denver Post*. "I picked up the paper and I was walking back into my gate and I was going to shut the iron gate and somebody hollered. It sounded like he said, 'Happy Fourth of July!' and I turned to see, and when I turned there was a car parked on the street, but I had a real big front yard. I saw the gun. He had a silk stocking over his face. I said to myself, 'OhmyGod, he's gonna shoot me!' The minute I said that, he did shoot me."[7]

Two of three shots hit her, one bullet passing through her back from left to right and another hitting her in the right leg. She said then and she maintains that she didn't recognize the shooter or the driver, or why they targeted her. "To this day, I don't know." Whoever it was, police concluded he wasn't a professional. It was, said an investigator, "an emotional type crime. If they wanted to be sure, they could have walked fifty feet and shot her again."[8] Family members had their suspect: Chauncey's second wife, Jeannie.

Whoever winged Pauline wasn't done with her. The front of her house was ripped apart by a dynamite explosion shortly after midnight on January 10, 1974, while she was watching television with a friend and the friend's daughter. "They weren't fifteen feet away from the blast. I don't know how they didn't get hurt," marveled an investigator.[9] Pauline had had enough. "When they bombed the house I never went back. I just fixed up the house and sold it."

Pauline Smaldone's home in Lakewood, a Denver suburb, was partially destroyed by a midnight explosion in 1974. She and two friends escaped without injury. © *The Denver Post*

Finally, there was Judy.

In the 1960s, Judy Good was a successful owner of racing dogs that ran at local tracks and, for a brief period, she owned stock in Interstate Kennel Club in Byers, Colorado. She and Young Eugene Smaldone started dating when they were twenty, and they were among three dozen people arrested in an after-hours club, what police called "a bawdy house," in Denver's Five Points neighborhood.

In 1968, because of her connections with the Smaldones and theirs with gambling, all of them, including Clyde, Checkers, Chauncey, and Paulie, were banned for life from the state's four dog and two horse tracks by the Colorado Racing Commission. A judge struck down the ban a few months later, ruling that there was no evidence any of them violated regulations governing conduct of patrons at the tracks. Young Eugene was banned again in 1972, after another gambling conviction and because he failed to pay $13,710 in outstanding fines on federal drug convictions. That ban was lifted in 1985 when he convinced the racing commission that he had to drive Judy to the dog track because she had an unspecified illness. And, he added for good measure, "I don't go to the track just to bet every night. I really enjoy just watching the dogs run."[10]

In 1976, while Young Eugene was in his fourth year of a ten-year sentence at federal penitentiaries in Leavenworth, Kansas, and La Tuna, Texas, on a cocaine-importing rap, Judy got married in a most unusual outdoor ceremony at Denver's historic Cheesman Park. A professed member of the Anton La Vey witch's coven, she exchanged vows with Lawrence Hamilton before a county judge on August 13, a Friday. She and the groom wore black, she carried black

Judy Good looked like a model when she met Young Eugene, but drugs stole her beauty before she died in 1998. © Colorado Historical Society, *The Denver Post,* September 13, 1963

roses, and she was given away by a man known to those in attendance only as Warlock Chuck.[11]

Young Eugene was paroled in 1978, Judy divorced her coven husband, and Smaldone and Judy lived together as husband and wife until, her beauty ravaged by drug abuse, Judy died on November 29, 1998.

# A Second Mob War

It felt like the Roaring Twenties all over again. Shoot-'em-up and blow-'em-up were back in style and no one, not even Smaldone family members, was safe. Rumblings surfaced early in 1963 of trouble in Denver's gambling community when police went public with a warning that syndicates, crippled by new federal laws against interstate gambling, were squeezing some of their business clients who failed to pay their debts. Police said in August that "at least a dozen" men were beaten.

Denver district attorney Bert Keating, admitting he'd only heard "wild rumors" about beatings and intimidation, was stymied in his investigations because no one wanted to sign a complaint. Police Chief Harold Dill was more sanguine about the apparent outbreak of violence. "None of these people was kidnapped and forced to gamble. They went there on their own."[1]

Not since the shoot-first days of the 1920s, when at least thirty members of the Danna, Carlino, and Roma gangs were gunned down in Denver and Pueblo, had the city seen so many mob-related deaths. Not that there hadn't been unsolved murders in the recent past. In 1948, gambler and self-styled tough guy Mike "Fats" Falbo, thirty, was found hanging out of the blood-spattered passenger-side door of his automobile in a roadside ditch near Welby, north of Denver. He'd been stabbed in the face numerous times and shot in the head three times. In 1950, Falbo's frequent gambling

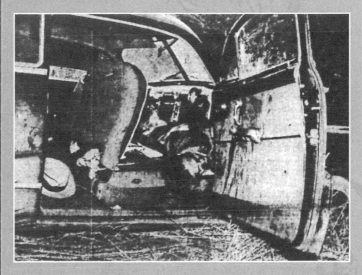

Gambler and tough guy Mike "Fats" Falbo sprawls across the front seat of his blood-splattered car after he was stabbed and shot to death © Colorado Historical Society, *The Denver Post*, January 8, 1948

companion and friend Harold "Murph" Cohen, thirty-five, was found by two boys under five feet of water near the shoreline of Blue Lake (now Coors Lake) near West Forty-fourth Avenue and McIntyre Street in rural Jefferson County. His hands and feet were trussed with wire and rope holding sixty pounds of railroad iron to his body and a large rock lashed to his midsection.

On August 7, 1963, a facile young mob novice named Robin Roberts, known on the street as Walkie-Talkie, turned up dead. Some said he got his nickname because he was a police informant, but those who knew him said it was because he was a compulsive talker. "Maybe it was just his way of being friendly, but he was always horning into conversations," said an acquaintance.

The thirty-two-year-old Roberts, his face bruised and three bullets in his chest, was found lying in a ditch in the fashionable Applewood Mesa subdivision outside Denver. A small-time gambler with modest means—he lived in the not-so-fashionable Kenmark Hotel downtown and drove a seven-year-old Chevy convertible—Roberts had a string of arrests for gambling and extortion.

He also had an annoying habit of failing to pay his gambling debts. "A welsher and a blabbermouth," said one insider. Various theories were floated about his murder: that he owed money to bookmakers in Canada and New York, that an outraged husband caught up with him, or that he snitched to the cops. Members of the Smaldone mob were called in for questioning, but police settled on one suspect, Sam Shanks, a St. Louis hoodlum brought in, they said, to kill Roberts. Shanks went to trial on a very shaky case—even the district attorney admitted it was largely circumstantial—and was acquitted. When the verdict was read, Shanks walked out of the courtroom, took a cab to the airport, and headed for Las Vegas, vowing never to come back. His farewell words: "I don't like Colorado."[2]

Roberts's fate had been sealed when, during his trial on interstate gambling charges, Denver detective Duane "Red" Borden, an organized-crime investigator who hounded the Smaldones for years, took the stand to testify and was ordered by the judge to reveal the name of his informant. He gave up Roberts. Retired Denver police captain Jerry Kennedy remembered, "I ran into Walkie a day or two later in that Theater Bar on Sixteenth and Glenarm, doing a routine check, and I said, 'How you doing, Walkie?' He says, 'Hey, Kennedy, they're going to kill me.' I said, 'Walkie, they're not going to kill you.' He says, 'Hey, I'm telling you, Borden named me on the stand. They're going to kill me.'"

Kennedy offered him police protection, but Roberts declined. "By God, within twenty-four hours they found this guy's body. My heart sunk into my stomach," Kennedy said.[3]

In 1973, three weeks after Pauline Smaldone was shot, John "Skip" LaGuardia, a handsome and personable former football lineman at the University of Colorado, was shotgunned in his front yard a few blocks from Chauncey and Pauline's Lakewood home. If any evidence was needed that things were heating up, this was it. "A lot of gamblers do more than gamble. They also kill people," observed a cop on the case.[4] The only apparent connection between the two shootings was the fact that the victims' homes were a few blocks apart in Lakewood.

LaGuardia, thirty, was a well-liked young man, president of his class at Mount Carmel High School, who first came to the attention of the legal system when he was caught distributing football parlay cards on the University of Colorado campus. He was kicked off the football team and quit school one semester short of graduation. Said one investigator who followed his brief career, "Skip had everything he needed to make it big—intelligence, the personality, the ambition. He would have been good at anything he tried. Anything, that is, but gangster."[5]

LaGuardia began to believe that gambling in Denver didn't have to be the exclusive realm of the Smaldones. He had big ambitions. One who knew him well and shared his bookmaking career was his friend and barber Jerry Middleton. "Skip was smart. He was the finest young guy you'd ever want to know. I'm just happy being myself [but] Skip wanted to be somebody. [He] just kept getting in deeper, deeper, deeper."[6] It came to a head when LaGuardia, with his pal Ralph Pizzalato at his side, called a senior member of the Denver underworld—insiders said it was Checkers—"an old man" and told him, "I don't need you anymore."[7] Another account of the confrontation had him slapping Checkers. Either way, it was a serious misstep.

Shortly after 1 AM on July 26, 1973, LaGuardia drove home from the Alpine Inn, 3551 Tejon Street, two blocks from Gaetano's and a hangout for gamblers and other gang and drug figures. He parked his car in the driveway and started up the walk to the house. He never got there. Somebody lying in wait stepped out of the bushes and shot him with a sawed-off 12-gauge shotgun, which the killer left beside the body.

A single pellet severed the left jugular vein in his neck and he bled to death. It was "a professional job" said police. "Let's put it this way," said an investigator. "They knew what they were doing. A gun like this can only be used to kill someone."[8]

Pizzalato, who some believed pulled the trigger on Skip LaGuardia, met his end six months later. On January 30, Pizzalato, his body in the fetal position in the backseat of his Cadillac, was found in the parking lot behind the Alpine with a gunshot to his left temple and signs of being choked.

Jay Whearley and John Toohey, who covered organized crime for *The Post*, followed the murders of LaGuardia and Pizzalato closely. Based on information from police sources, they wrote that the men's deaths and the two attempts on Pauline Smaldone were "connected with the victims' attempts to form their own bookmaking and criminal operation," which would have drawn money away from established syndicates. Pauline maintains she barely knew LaGuardia and never met Pizzalato. None of the cases was ever solved.

Alone with his memories, an aging Clyde Smaldone enjoys a beer at the far end of the bar at Gaetano's, a spot he occupied frequently through the years. © Smaldone Family Collection

# CHAPTER SIXTEEN

# RECESSIONAL

*I never thought it would end.*

—Clyde Smaldone

When Clyde and Checkers returned to Denver in November 1962 after serving nine and a half years for federal jury tampering, Clyde was ready to put the past behind him and begin a legitimate career. He told *The Denver Post* that he might try to get back to running Gaetano's, "provided the authorities let me, which I think they will. They've been pretty nice."[1]

It should have been a happy period, but family ties were coming loose.

Clyde warned other members of the gambling operation that it was time for them to get out of the business too. He recognized that the law-enforcement landscape was changing. The FBI, with the help of local police departments, was cracking down on interstate gambling and devoting more resources to fighting organized crime. The chase went on twenty-four hours a day, seven days a week. Crimes that once resulted in ninety days in jail and a fine of a few hundred dollars now were punished with several years in a federal penitentiary. Getting betting odds from out of state, which the Smaldone syndicate did, was now a federal offense. Wiretaps were everywhere. "My dad was smart," recalled his son Gene. "He used to tell Chauncey and Paulie. He told them, 'They [the police] are setting you up. They know what you guys are doing.' They wouldn't listen to Dad, partly because he was drinking and partly because they didn't want to. He didn't have as much control anymore."[2]

But he had enough control that he could still flash his street-tough side. After Clyde helped organize a union for restaurant workers with Mike Pomponio , who owned a restaurant not far from Gaetano's, Pomponio told him, "Clyde, the union, you know what they're going to do? They're gonna picket the place. Can you get ahold of them?" Clyde met with a union representative and told him, "When you come here tomorrow, over [to] Pomponio's or me, bring six ambulances with you, four doctors, then you can come over and picket, [because] that's what's going to happen if you come here." Nobody showed up.

Having "retired" from his former life of crime, Clyde was ready to look to the future, but he couldn't forgive Checkers, whose fault it was that both men wound up at Leavenworth on jury-tampering charges. "We went to jail, that beloved brother of mine, Checkers. I spent my money and I asked him to pay me the money I spent. I done nine and a half years of my life for him. He won't even pay me the money he owes me. If you call that a good brother...

"And not only me. The other six, seven guys that tried to help him—some of them had to hock their house, some of them lost business, lost their jobs, and to this day he's never given one of them guys a quarter. Like he didn't me, and I was his brother."

The rift created two factions within the family, who, even if they weren't working against each other, weren't working together as they had for forty years. One group consisted of Chauncey, Paulie Villano, and Clyde, and the other group was made up of Joe Salardino; Checkers's son, Young Eugene; and, when he came back from prison after serving brief sentences for gambling in 1972 and 1974, Checkers himself. Clyde remained bitter. "A lot of times I got to thinking, because I wasn't guilty of really, really being involved…with my brother [Checkers]. I shouldn't have even tried to help him because he's a no good s.o.b."

To make matters worse, Clyde's drinking was becoming problematic. Mark Valente, whose father, Ray, ran Valente's restaurant in Wheat Ridge, a hangout for the Smaldones and their associates, remembered that Clyde and his son Gene, who tried to keep him away from alcohol, frequently visited the bar in Marc's restaurant, across the street from Valente's. "On the way to the bathroom, the pay phone was there. He'd tell [the bartender] to put the shot glasses with whiskey there. So he'd walk to the bathroom and he'd do a shot, then he'd come back and sit at the bar and talk to Gene, go to the bathroom again, do another shot."[3] On one occasion, he went to get the drink, only to discover that someone else had consumed it.

At one point, he was drinking twelve short bottles of Hamm's beer, his favorite, a day. "Clyde and me went drinking every morning," sometimes starting at eight in the morning, remembered Joe Valley, who moved up from Pueblo and lived in an apartment above Gaetano's for a decade and did odd jobs, including driving Clyde and Checkers around. "And he drank whiskey. I know because I bought it at the liquor store for him when he wanted it. When we got to his house, he poured it into one of them mixing bowls and said, 'Now you take this empty bottle. Don't throw it around here. Take it and throw it in [Gaetano's] trash.'"[4] "After four or five years of this, [Clyde's son] Gene gives me a call one day. 'I don't want you "treating" my dad anymore.'" Clyde took it out on Joe. "I said, 'You talk it over with your son. He's the one who told me not to take you.'"[5] Trying to stem the booze tide, Gene and Chuck put their father in treatment on more than one occasion. Once, they tricked him into going to rehab by plying him with beers.

His worsening habit made him less and less accessible to other members of the mob, and they paid less attention to his opinions. Checkers became the de facto head man.

But Checkers, too, was no longer the dominating figure he had once been. As he sat in the back of police squad car after an arrest for gambling in 1974, a *Post* reporter described him: "Wearing the kind of clothing—including a wide-brimmed straw hat—that any old man might wear when he works in his yard or drinks a beer in his neighborhood tavern, the man sits and glares at everyone peering in at him."[6] A curious rookie cop, when told who the man in the backseat was, "That's Checkers? I always thought he was a younger guy."[7]

Clyde's legacy following his release from his last trip to prison was his warning to other family members that their heyday had passed. They ignored him. What were they going to do, launch new careers? Checkers was fifty-three, Chauncey thirty-nine, and Paulie Villano thirty-five. Gambling was the only livelihood they knew. The three continued to run parlay cards and give high-interest loans, racking up dozens of arrests in the 1970s and 1980s.

Arrested in 1974, sixty-three-year-old Checkers Smaldone became
a curiosity seated in a police car. One officer commented, "That's
Checkers? I thought he was a younger guy." © *The Denver Post*

The FBI finally crushed the mob in 1981 when a bug planted in the tiny office in Gaetano's basement caught a seriocomic conversation between Villano, Checkers, and Valley about the inner workings of a silencer. To the untrained ear, it sounded like an Abbott and Costello comedy routine.

Paul Villano: See, Joe, when you look through this, it looks like it goes all the way.

Joe Valley: I bet you if we get a long rod, see if it's really straight...

Checkers Smaldone: I don't want nobody puttin' no rods in there.

Villano: Stick it through here?

Smaldone: What for?

Villano: Just to see...'Cuz that little thing will deflect the bullet. Just like you hit a limb on a tree, it'll deflect the bullet.

Smaldone: Just tell me, how's the bullet gonna get through this hole after it leaves the tunnel?

Valley: It'll go straight.

Villano: Well, we'll try it. I just hate to blow that sonofabitch apart. Too bad we don't know nobody that knows about them. Joe, let me ask you something. Did the book that you read say it had to be packed all the way through?[8]

The outcome was less hilarious. In August, the FBI and Denver police conducted a series of raids in Denver and Pueblo and confiscated a silencer, a .30-caliber carbine and twenty-seven rounds of ammunition, four handguns, and stacks of documents. They also seized $50,000 in cash hidden in the restaurant.

Valley went to trial and was acquitted, but Checkers Smaldone and Villano pleaded guilty and were convicted of loan-sharking, income-tax evasion, and firearms violations. Chauncey, who missed the basement discussion about a silencer because he had been hospitalized for tests, was convicted on similar charges. All three received ten-year sentences. Many predicted that the men, especially Checkers, wouldn't live out their time.

*Rocky Mountain News* reporter Bill Gallo wrote a slice-of-life profile of Checkers, then seventy-two, in 1982, during a farewell stop at Gaetano's while waiting to begin his last prison sentence. Gallo captured the onetime tough-guy image:

> Through the afternoon, Checkers had been receiving, amid a thick cloud of smoke emanating from his huge Nicaraguan Emperador, a succession of long-term business associates, ancient neighborhood friends with rumpled felt hats stuck onto their heads and well-wishers who spoke quietly and carried their hats in their hands. By the time the parade was over, Checkers had knocked off 10 or 12 neat cognacs and offered to take either team in that night's World Series game.[9]

On his last day on Earth, March 17, 1992, Checkers Smaldone called his best fishing and drinking buddy, Joe

Valley, who picked him up at noon. "We went around, drank," Valley recalled. At 6 PM, a weary Checkers said, "I guess you'd better take me to the hospital," where he was scheduled to undergo colon cancer surgery. Less than two hours later, Checkers died of a heart attack in his bed at St. Anthony Central Hospital. He was eighty-one.

Clyde's world was shrinking. He'd dropped out of the family's bookmaking and loan-sharking operations in 1962. His brother Checkers, with whom he had fought the mob wars, gone to prison with, and feuded with, was dead. Mildred, his wife of sixty-five years, died in March 1993 after more than a decade in a nursing home, where Clyde visited her almost every day, no matter the weather. When she was interred at Crown Hill Cemetery, he continued to visit often, sitting in a big easy chair next to her crypt and talking to her.

Several years before his death, Clyde Smaldone underwent a transformation. He quit drinking—more than once before he made it stick. Raised in a religious family, Clyde had gone, briefly, to a Catholic school. He talked often about his religious upbringing and was legendary in the neighborhood for his donations to Catholic charities. In time, he had drifted away from Catholicism, but remained a religious man. The building and dedication of Mount Carmel High School, which he helped finance in the 1950s, was the straw that broke Clyde's ties with the church. When Clyde, Checkers, and their friends raised $50,000 to build the school in North Denver, one of the men they went to for a donation was their attorney Anthony Zarlengo. Late in his life, Clyde said, "We says, 'We want you to donate some money to help build.' He says, 'Oh I don't believe in nothing like that. I don't believe in doing that.' They got the school built, and who do you think they brought to cut the ribbon to open the school? It was Anthony Zarlengo! I was there [and] I says, 'You ain't gonna let that man...' The cops come and pulled me away. They let him cut the ribbon, but I never respected the Catholic Church from then on."

Clyde became a born-again Christian, thanks to Dee Claxton, whose sister, Mary, was Gene Smaldone's second wife. Like other prominent men, as his days wound down Clyde began to think beyond this life. He was fond of telling people, "When I die and go to hell, Hitler and I are going to run hell."

Claxton, one of many who chauffeured Clyde because he had an aversion to driving, worried at first what she and the retired mobster would talk about on their trips. She quickly learned that the Kennedys, Barbara Walters, and Jane Fonda were fire starters. Born again herself, she began to engage Clyde in discussions about religion. "He was really questioning me about it. Bless his heart, he had given this a lot of thought over the years, and he prayed out loud in the car and gave his heart to Jesus."[10] Later, he called her and said, "Y'know, until I met you and your sister, I didn't know that Jesus loved me."

His health failing, Clyde spent his remaining days at Lutheran Nursing Home, but even there he tried to stay in charge, telling other residents where and when they could sit for meals in the communal dining room. Old friends stopped by and sometimes took him for a drive, with ample instruction from Clyde. If he was to be picked up at 9:00, his ride better be there at 9:00 or face getting an irate phone call. He asked Gene for money, despite having nowhere to spend it. Having it, as in the old days, was what mattered. Sometimes he'd have $500 in his shirt pocket. He worked on his Christian attitude, though he sometimes snapped at those helping him, "I had better haircuts in prison" or "I had better food in prison." He also made it a point to hand out Hershey's chocolate bars to the residents and caretakers.

Clyde Smaldone, the man who had his first brush with the law as a thirteen-year-old in 1920, became friends with presidents and mobsters, and spent thousands of dollars on lawyers and charitable causes, died at ninety-one on January 7, 1998. His friends remembered him warmly. At the end of the reading of the eulogy at the Crown Hill Cemetery chapel, those in attendance stood and applauded.

That left only Chauncey and Paulie. Chauncey, his memory fogged from time to time by dementia, continued to frequent Gaetano's, which, on bad days, he believed he still owned, despite the fact that it had been sold to a restaurant group headed by Denver's mayor. He would call family members, then call them again, forgetting that he had called only minutes before. Not long before his death, he suffered a heart attack. As a final insult, his wife, Jeannie, dropped him off at Gaetano's one Friday morning and disappeared. When she didn't come back for him, a Gaetano's employee called police, who had him admitted to a hospital. Without explanation, Jeannie turned up the following Tuesday. It was left to Chauncey's first wife, Pauline, and her children to care for him until time ran out.

When the last Smaldone brother died in hospice on

October 16, 2006, at eighty-two, with his children by his side, the family kept the news a secret for a month and there was no public funeral; they didn't want Jeannie, the woman they all despised, to find out that he was dead. His body was cremated, and his children had a private service in his memory with family and friends one month later. Pauline still keeps his ashes.

For his part, Paulie labored on in the family crime vineyard, getting arrested periodically on minor bookmaking and loan-sharking charges. He once was busted conducting business in a phone booth across the street from Gaetano's and promptly ate the betting slips. Gambling became a low priority for police, who were busy trying to keep a lid on street gangs and drug trafficking, just as they had done with bootleggers and their illicit liquor forty years earlier. When his ten-year prison sentence ended in 1991, Villano returned to Denver and kept a low profile. Plagued by arthritis in his hips and shoulders, a remnant of his days as a gymnast, he developed a virulent infection, fell into a coma, and died at the age of seventy-six on November 12, 2003.

With his death, the era of the Smaldone crime syndicate came to a quiet and unspectacular conclusion. At the end of his life, Clyde always gave the same reply when asked why he didn't invest the millions that flowed through the family's hands: "I never thought it would end."

Nine-year-old Chuck Smaldone and his friend Smokey Bear sit for a family portrait with Chuck's parents, Mildred and Clyde, in their North Denver home in 1954. © Smaldone Family Collection

# EPILOGUE

*We were an Italian family, just like any other family.*

—Gene Smaldone

The Smaldones' reputation as Mafia-style mobsters in big hats and wide-lapel suits racing around Denver and gunning down rivals endures, even today. Pictures of them exiting a courtroom, their faces obscured by a hat or a hand, were frequently in the newspapers from the 1940s to the 1980s. Everybody knew who they were. Rumors about whom they had killed or roughed up for nonpayment of gambling debts persist, and they were referred to, wrongly, in the 1950s as "one of the strongest and most powerful Mafia machines in the country."[1] "The Smaldones were the biggest in Denver, Colorado," says onetime bookmaker Jerry Middleton. "There wasn't anybody else. Nobody had their charisma, nobody else did what they did."[2]

In the greater mob galaxy, the Smaldones were a small planet, isolated in mid-America. They were no angels, but their exploits pale in comparison to the popular image of the Godfather movies or *The Sopranos* television series, or even when measured against the hard-core mobs in New Orleans, Chicago, New York, Kansas City, and Miami. Local police sometimes dismissed them as small potatoes, except when they arrested them, because they knew the Smaldones were front-page news.

They had star power. Many people claim to have known Clyde, Checkers, and the rest. Few did. They knew the public side but not the private side. In addition to their public "mob" persona, they are still recalled fondly in the North Denver neighborhood for their willingness to help families in need, whether it was with food during the Great Depression or projects that needed funding. In this, Clyde and Checkers followed an age-old tradition among gamblers. Horace Greeley, editor of the *New York Tribune*, toured the West in 1859 and visited embryonic Denver, then only months old. In a series of thirty-four letters for the *Tribune*, he wrote:

> As a class, the gamblers were entertaining in conversation, had curious experiences to relate, evinced great knowledge of human nature, and were especially kind to each other in misfortune. Some were gentlemanly in manners. Like all men who gain money easily, they were open-handed and charitable. I never saw a place where more dollars could be obtained in less time for helpless women or orphans than among gaming tables.[3]

In today's world, where gambling, high credit-card interest rates, and liquor are legal, the Smaldones, particularly Clyde, might have become successful businessmen instead of making their living in gambling, loan-sharking, and bootlegging. Their illegal business interests aside, they lived by their word, disdained drugs and prostitution, and even in their dealings with law enforcement, conducted themselves as gentlemen. "I couldn't say anything bad about Clyde," said former Denver police captain Larry Britton, who, after he left the department, drove the aging mobster around in his last days. "The way he talked like a Republican conservative. He was really down on dope and prostitution." On the other hand, Britton said, "You gotta understand when these people say [gambling] was a victimless crime [that] we used to get calls from housewives, 'Hey, my husband...Why don't you guys go break this up? They're spending all the money. I can't go to the grocery store, I can't pay my rent.' Used to happen all the time."[4]

As the Smaldones and their crowd aged, their power, influence, and notoriety diminished. In the extended family of cousins, aunts, and uncles, the name was sometimes kept under wraps. Some members changed their last name; others refuse to acknowledge their heritage. In any case, the weight of the Smaldone name was obvious. Louis Smaldone, a nephew, recalled that when he got out of the army, he took a job as a floorwalker for Neusteter's, an upscale department store in Denver. "I had to wear a suit and a boutonniere, but they said, 'Whatever you do, your name is "Mr. Lou." Do not bring up the Smaldone name at all.' Anytime anybody had to get a signature or something like that, they'd call for 'Mr. Lou,' and that was me. I did that for about six or eight months and got out of there."[5]

Except for Checkers's son, Young Eugene, the next generation stayed out of the family business. Gene went into teaching and coaching; Chuck became a purveyor of high-end men's clothing. Louis Smaldone became a successful real-estate investor. Pauline and Chauncey's offspring, Paul Michael and Claudia Jean (named for her Uncle Clyde), went into the vending machine business and law, respectively. Never married, Paulie Villano had no children.

In the end, the Smaldone empire, at its peak in the 1950s, couldn't last. Retired Denver police captain Jerry Kennedy says of the dichotomy: "Comparatively, these guys were amateurs, in a sense because they had two problems: one, they couldn't recruit, they didn't have the Italian community here to recruit from, and they kept their own families out of it, so the bottom line was that it was destined to die."[6]

Coinciding with the diminishing Smaldone power, their North Denver enclave changed. Gone are the days when a youthful Gene, Chauncey, Ralph, and Paulie wandered the neighborhood on their homemade scooters, dug caves in the empty lots, and built spook houses in their garages. Gone too are Clyde's giant banana splits, called super-dupers by the boys.

It was a neighborhood where, during Prohibition, residents left their garage doors open so bootleggers fleeing police could pull in and hide. Or, if a young man was in a scrape with a pursuing officer, he could sit down on a stranger's porch with the woman of the house as though he had been there the whole time.

In the early part of the twentieth century, North Denver was a separate entity, with its own grocery stores, bakeries, bars, and restaurants. But the story of the Italian migration out of the neighborhood is a familiar one. As their lives and finances improved, Italians began the slow trek up the social ladder, out of the Bottoms near the South Platte River, up the bluffs to Highlands to the north and west, and, beginning in the 1950s, to the suburbs of Arvada,

Wheat Ridge, and Lakewood, leaving in their wake the next wave of immigrants, from Latin America. Today there are Hispanic-run stores in North Denver where businesses once sported the Italian names Canino, Aiello, Rotola, and Carbone. Gaetano's restaurant, on the same corner for more than sixty years, has as its neighbors El Vaquero Joyeria, Marco's Mexican Corner, and Video Mexico. The transition of the neighborhood can be seen at Columbus Park, West Thirty-eighth Avenue and Navajo Street, called La Raza Park by Hispanics.

But the Smaldone name lives on, the good and bad, inside and outside the neighborhood.

Chuck Smaldone leans forward in his chair and, with his best faux Italian accent, says, "My name is Carlos Raffaele Paulae Smaldon-ay." Born in Denver in 1945, Clyde Smaldone's second son knows better than anyone the baggage behind the name.

Fifteen years younger than his brother Gene, Chuck grew up in his only sibling's shadow. "My brother was always a good athlete, and I could walk across the room and fall ten times tripping over my own feet. You know, my brother will say no, but he was every father's dream of a son. He was a football player; he was nice looking. He won't say, but all the girls liked him, he did good in school, never had any problems, so what father wouldn't want to have him as a son? I was the opposite. I couldn't walk across the room without falling over. I wasn't very good-looking."[7]

Gene's difficulties with the Smaldone legacy came later. As a kid, he was adept at math, starred as a running back at North High School, then went on to play on a very good football team at the University of Denver between 1949 and 1951, where his teammates included high school coaching legend Fred Tesone and NFL/Canadian Football League quarterback Sam Etcheverry. His career in athletics shielded him. "Nobody ever said anything to me. Now, it was different with my brother. I never noticed the name Smaldone meant anything. It really never came up. I started playing Young America League football, so I was always involved in that. Nobody at school ever bothered me."[8]

The same could not be said for Chuck. His father, he says, "was a good dad," but Clyde was absent, at federal prison in Leavenworth, Kansas, during Chuck's formative years, between 1955 and 1962, when he matured from a boy of ten to a young man of seventeen. There was a void. "I can remember when my dad left and he said, 'Son, you are the man of the house now. You have to take care of Mother.' I never forgot that."

The unkind cuts began early. Chuck was a retiring, skinny kid, "a nerd" in his words. "I remember one time I was in grade school. I think maybe I was, like, third or fourth or fifth grade. They called [on] me, and one of the teachers made a crack about my name and that I was a gangster's son. I remember that was the first time, and the kids all kind of laughed. That was always in the back of my mind, and I was absolutely mortified."

It didn't help that his mother picked him up from school in the family's Cadillac, usually the current year's model, eliciting sniggers from his classmates. "I told her if she'd ever pick me up I'd make her meet me away from the school so nobody would see that I was in a fancy car. One time she came when I was in junior high, she came for parent-teacher conferences. My mom always used to dress nice, and [the teacher] saw my mom pull up in a Cadillac and she said, 'You know, not everybody can afford a Cadillac automobile. I guess you must be pretty wealthy people.' My mother had no formal education, but she was a very wise person. She said, 'Well, that's not the measure of somebody's quality or what their value is.'"

Despite all this, Chuck proved as smart as his older brother, following him to the University of Denver, where he was in the honors program in sociology. Until health problems forced him into early retirement, he enjoyed a successful career as a men's clothier in Arvada, an occupation that gave him another reason to admire his father: an insider's appreciation of Clyde's fine taste in clothes. "Dad, out of all the brothers, used to be the best dresser when he was younger. He used to wear Chester Barrie suits that started at $300. Today, they would be $5,000. He used to wear Bannister shoes. Those were English-made shoes and they were the best, and you get those only by special order."

His boyhood trauma aside, there was a larger skeleton in Chuck's cluttered closet: he is gay. In a world where machismo, exaggerated masculinity, and the mob mentality of tough guys reigned, it was a double burden for him, one he was terrified would be discovered. He ducked out the back doors of gay bars for fear his name might wind up in the newspaper after a police morals raid, not unheard of during his youthful days in Denver. He and his partner, Daniel Henry, a hospital statistician who also taught at

Regis University and Metropolitan State College, enjoyed a twenty-seven-year relationship until Henry's death from cancer in 1996.

His father, Chuck remembers, seemed okay with his sexual orientation, except when he'd been drinking. Embarrassment was part of his arsenal. "My dad used to have those dinners down at Gaetano's, and some married friends came one night with me. He knew she was married. I was sitting there with them, and my dad comes over and he says to her, "You know, I wish you'd really straighten my son out.' 'Clyde, what do you mean?' 'You know what I mean, straighten him out.' I said, 'Dad, this is her husband.' He was funny about things."

Pressures at school and fears about discovery of his sexual orientation finally boiled over when Chuck was sixteen. "I got to the point where I wouldn't go to school. I hated to go to school. My mom used to have tranquilizers and sleeping pills, and I took one or two every week until I had enough saved up that I thought would do it.

"Aunt Pauline and Uncle Chauncey came over for dinner that night and I had a nice dinner and I thought, well, this was a nice evening, so I took the pills and I can remember going to my bed and laying down and feeling the greatest relief that you could possibly feel. I felt like a thousand pounds had been lifted off my shoulders. I just fell off to sleep."

It wasn't to be, thanks to his father. "My dad got sick that night and he got up to go to the bathroom and he walked by my room. For some strange reason, he turned on the light in my bedroom. I was blue. I had stopped breathing. My dad threw a cold cloth on my face, and I gasped for air. They took me to the hospital, and they did this tracheotomy out on the street." It was a narrow escape. Chuck lay in a coma for three days, his father and mother at his bedside almost the entire time.

Chuck had a hard time separating from his mother and father, who, like many Italian parents, were eager to keep their son at home, even after he graduated from high school and was old enough to attend the University of Denver across town. He wanted to rent an apartment; they fixed up the basement so he could live at home. Clyde offered him a deal. "'If you come home, just for the summer, I'll buy you a new car.' I said, 'Just for the summer, Dad? Okay, deal.' They just didn't want me to leave. The next thing out of their mouths: 'Don't you like us anymore?'" Eventually, he did move into an apartment near the campus.

The separation became final in his late twenties, when he declared his homosexuality. "That was a very difficult time in my life, when I made the decision to come out. I was very lucky and I met a nice group of fellows and we all used to hang out together. We all had jobs, were professional people. We were stable. Three of them were decorated Vietnam War veterans."

Once Chuck's older brother, Clean Gene (a designation he dislikes, even though it is used to differentiate him from his drug-abusing cousin, Checkers's son Young Eugene), left his college life, he found that the Smaldone name hounded him, too. "I remember when I was growing up my mother telling me that if I did something wrong, the police would come down on me twice as hard as my friends. I didn't really think about it because I was so busy and everything was good for me and I was doing all the things I liked and was happy doing them. It didn't affect me much. Or at all."

He spent 1952 and 1953 coaching football in suburban Westminster High School at the same time his father was on trial for jury tampering. He took a better-paying job (he was making only $2,900 a year at Westminster) teaching elementary school in Denver so he could go to law school at night. "I thought, maybe, someday, I would be able to help my dad." It was at law school that he realized his name was working against him—"Some of the professors made it more difficult for me"—and he gave up on law in 1955 after two years of schooling. "I probably wouldn't have been happy being a lawyer," Gene said. "Plus, I was teaching school, going to school at night, carrying mail in the summer, and working at the dog track at night. And I was married and had two little daughters."

Gene and two equally financially strapped teacher friends, Jim Erfurdt and Gordon Phifer, in 1957 founded Summer Fun Day Camp, which took school-age children swimming, bowling, and to other activities. It became hugely successful, beginning with one bus and twenty-five kids a week and ballooning to thirty-six vans and more than six hundred participants. The camp's popularity led the partners to build their own swimming pool, called Swimland, in Wheat Ridge. Out of that came the partners' real-estate business, focusing on building and managing apartment buildings.

It took him eight years, but he finally landed an assistant coaching job at Lincoln High School in Denver in 1964 and served three years as head coach. One of his teams won

When Gene Smaldone, a football star at the University of
Denver, married Jean Veto in 1951, 1,500 well-wishers attended
at the Willow Springs Country Club. Gene's parents, Clyde and
Mildred, are at right. © Smaldone Family Collection

a city championship, but "I knew, because of my name, no matter how good a coach I could be, I would never get the opportunity to coach or referee at the college level because of my dad's involvement in gambling."

Gene is semiretired but continues to manage a number of properties. He wed three times, for the first time in 1951, when he married Jean. The reception at the now-defunct Willow Springs Country Club outside Denver was the social event of the season and several seasons to follow. More than 1,500 guests, including friends, football players, reporters, politicians, police officers, lawyers, and Smaldone cohorts showed up. Newspaper photographers recorded it all, like the wedding celebration right out of *The Godfather*. They had four daughters—Debbie, Linda, Paula, and Suzie—but, sadly, Jean, bedeviled by depression, committed suicide in 1970. His second wife, Mary, whom he married in 1974, died of cancer in 1988. He has been married to Linda, his present wife, since 1991.

The Smaldones' notoriety continued to follow the siblings. When Gene was teaching at school one day, FBI agents banged on his front door at home, showed their badges, and demanded that his terrified teenage daughters tell them where he was. It turned out the agents were at the wrong house and were looking for Checkers, who lived several miles away. No apology was forthcoming until Gene threatened to go to the newspapers with the story. Another time, the IRS spent three years and thousands of dollars probing his business finances. He ultimately paid $300 in additional taxes.

Both men continue to deal with "name recognition." A check or a credit card often brings the reaction, "Oh, are you related to those Smaldones?" "When I say yes," says Gene, "they don't know what to say next."

Growing up, the boys lived in a family that was like any other, albeit an Italian family where no Italian was spoken because their mother, Mildred, was of German-Irish descent. Clyde frequently attended Gene's football games at the University of Denver and often treated the entire team to postgame meals at Gaetano's. Their mother went to school functions, cared for the boys by herself when Clyde was serving time, and made sure they stayed away from the family business. "My dad was never real show-offy," says Gene. "He used to dress nice, but he never had watches or rings or anything like that. My mom was a wonderful mother. I think she kept it separated."

The brothers made long car or train trips with their mother to visit their dad when he was serving time at Leavenworth. They'd travel 600 miles for a three-hour stay. Prison rules allowed only one visit per month, so they scheduled their visits on the last day of the month and the first day of the following month. Then the rules were changed to thirty days between visits, and they visited when they could. Mildred wrote to Clyde almost every day, and Chuck wrote when she didn't, because mail for prisoners was restricted.

Dozens of his letters, still preserved by the family, were Chuck's connection to his father about everyday life. In 1956, when he was eleven, he wrote, in part:

Dear Daddy,                    July 21, 1906

How are you? I am fine.
T.V. is on now. It is about
5 of 10 o'clock now daddy. Today
is Jean's birthday, and we
went to Elitches tonight daddy.
I fished at Elitches and one time
I pulled up four fish on one
hook, all togeather. I have 12
airplanes that I won. In a
month and a half before school
starts daddy. We will be down
to see you soon daddy. We were
up to Margaret's daddy for
about 3 days daddy. I miss you
very much daddy. Do you miss
me daddy? I love you very
much daddy. I hope you come
home soon daddy. Here are
some kiss an hags.
OOOOOOOOOOOOOO  X X X
X X   X X X X X X X X   X   X X

                              Love
                              Chuck

P.S Look on the other side SURprise ➡

Chuck Smaldone, who became "the man of the family" when Clyde
went to Leavenworth for ten years, wrote frequently to his father,
who saved all of his letters. © Smaldone Family Collection

How are you? I am fine. T.V. is on now. It is about 5 of 10 oclock now daddy...In a month and a half before school starts daddy. We will be down to see you soon daddy...Do you miss me daddy? I love you very much daddy. I hope you come home soon daddy. Here are some kiss an hugs.

XXXXXXXXXXXXX/OOOOOOOOOOO OO/XXXXXXXXXXX.

Love, Chuck

On the back was a drawing of the Chuck Flying Saucer drive-in, marked "Good Food."

Their public persona aside, it was a different world inside the family. Dee Claxton, who helped Clyde find Jesus, remembered, "The more you hung out with the family, the more you realized they're just ordinary people, and nicer than most of us."[9]

"He was a very good dad," remembers Chuck. "I used to sit on his lap when I was three and four years old, and we used to watch television or listen to the radio. He was heavyset, and so his lap was kind of comfortable because he was fat, and he'd smoke his big cigars."

"My dad was good to everybody," says Gene. "If someone needed money, he'd give it to them." The son who went into coaching instead of the mob hits the heart of the matter: "People come out and say, 'Mafia.' We never heard the word *Mafia*. We were an Italian family, just like any other family."

# Notes

## Chapter One: Little Caesar

1. "Sobs Wrack Mrs. Joe Roma as She Tells of Slain Mate," *Rocky Mountain News*, February 19, 1933.
2. Ibid.
3. "Roma Slain as He Plays Mandolin in Home," *Rocky Mountain News*, February 19, 1933.
4. "$1,000 Display of Flowers Will Bank Casket of Joseph Roma at Elaborate Funeral Today," *Rocky Mountain News*, February 22, 1933.
5. "Joe Roma, Convicted as Liquor King, Claimed to Be Grocer," *The Denver Post*, February 19, 1933.
6. "Traitor Who Was Paid $100 Is Hunted as Slayer of Roma," *The Denver Post*, February 26, 1933.
7. "Roma Appears Voluntarily for Gangland Quiz," *The Denver Post*, May 13, 1931.
8. "Fourteen Bullets Strike Roma in Gun Volley," *The Denver Post*, February 19, 1933.
9. "That's That" column, *The Denver Post*, February 19, 1933.
10. "Vag 'em," *Rocky Mountain News*, February 26, 1933.
11. "Verdict in Smaldone Case Opens Way to Smash Denver Gangs," *The Denver Post*, February 25, 1933.
12. "Denver Hoodlums Denied Special Privilege in Jail," *The Denver Post*, February 28, 1933.
13. "Denver Gang Leaders Fight for Roma's Place," *The Denver Post*, December 26, 1932.

## Chapter Two: Arrivals

1. Thinkquest. "Immigration: The Journey to America: The Italians." http://library.thinkquest.org/20619/Italian.html.
2. Rebecca Ann Hunt, "Urban Pioneers: Continuity and Change in the Ethnic Communities in Two Denver, Colorado, Neighborhoods 1875–1998" (PhD dissertation, Univ. of Colorado History Department, 1999), 82.
3. Carlo Levi, *Christ Stopped at Eboli: The Story of a Year* (New York: Noonday Press, 1979), 121.
4. Thomas J. Noel. "The Immigrant Saloon in Denver," *Colorado Magazine* 54 (June 1977): 211.

5. Ibid.
6. Andrew Rolle, *Westward the Immigrants* (Niwot, CO: Univ. Press of Colorado, 1999), 22.
7. Christine A. DeRose, "Inside 'Little Italy': Italian Immigrants in Denver" *Colorado Magazine* 54 (June 1977): 283.
8. Ibid., 289.
9. Stephen J. Leonard, *Lynching in Colorado 1859–1919* (Niwot, CO: Univ. Press of Colorado, 2002), 135–139.
10. D. J. Cook, *Hands Up; Or, Twenty Years of Detective Life in the Mountains and the Plains* (Norman: Univ. of Oklahoma Press), 12–26.
11. DeRose, "Inside 'Little Italy,'" 279.

## CHAPTER THREE: BOOTLEG

1. "Police Open War to Drive Denver Gangs Out of City," *The Denver Post*, March 18, 1932.
2. Red Fenwick, "The Smaldone Story," pt. 2, *Roundup* magazine, *The Denver Post*, December 10, 1953.

## CHAPTER FOUR: NOBLE EXPERIMENT

1. Thomas J. Noel, *The City and the Saloon* (Niwot, CO: Univ. Press of Colorado, 1982), 114.
2. "Rare Wines from Club Cellars Go Cut Rate," *The Denver Times*, December 20, 1915.
3. "'Dry' Year Is Ushered in with Marked Quiet as Bars Close Early," *Rocky Mountain News*, January 1, 1916.
4. A. G. Birch, "Denver Drinks Health of New Year in Lemonade as Joy Liquids Vanish," *The Denver Post*, January 1, 1916.
5. "To Be Charged with Violation of Colorado's Prohibition Statute," *The Denver Times*, January 6, 1916.
6. "Girls No Longer Barred by Bars," *Rocky Mountain News*, January 3, 1916.
7. L. A. Chapin, "Brew Sold Over Bar as Thirsty Stampede Makes Its Own Laws," *The Denver Post*, April 7, 1933.
8. Robert Perkin, *The First Hundred Years* (New York: Doubleday, 1959), 450.
9. Frances Wayne, "2,006 Drunks in City in Year Prove Federal Dry Law Needed," *The Denver Post*, January 1, 1918.
10. Frances Wayne, "41 Denver Youths Made Blind by Moonshine Booze in Year," *The Denver Post*, September 19, 1923.
11. "Wets Win in Post Referendum," *The Denver Post*, February 23, 1926.
12. "Deport All Bootleg Foreigners, Urges Colorado's Dry Director," *The Denver Post*, October 9, 1921.
13. "Business Booms First 'Dry' Day," *Rocky Mountain News*, January 4, 1916.
14. "Post Punches," editorial, *The Denver Post*, July 21, 1925.

15. Bruce A. Gustin, "Liquor Crazed Crowds Ignore Law and Order," *The Denver Post*, December 11, 1933.
16. Jack Carberry, "Rubber Sandwich Outlawed in City Liquor Cleanup," *The Denver Post*, October 1, 1935.
17. Walden E. Sweet, "Guthner Issues Order Defining Minimum Meal," *The Denver Post*, December 11, 1935.
18. L. A. Chapin, "Denver Ready to Make Sky Ring in Rousing Welcome to President," *The Denver Post*, November 6, 1932.

## Chapter Five: Murder, Inc.

1. Phil Goodstein, *In the Shadow of the Klan: When the KKK Ruled Denver 1920–1926* (Denver: New Social Publications, 2006), 19.
2. Ibid.
3. Ibid., 22.
4. "Detective Klein Killed from Ambush/Body of Officer Riddled by Buckshot," *The Denver Post*, August 29, 1919.
5. "Coward," editorial, *The Denver Post*, August 29, 1919.
6. "Plot of Southern Colorado Gang to Invade Denver Found," *The Denver Post*, January 24, 1931.
7. "There Ain't No Crime in Denver," *The Denver Post*, May 10, 1931.
8. "Four More Men Taken in Drive on 'Rum Trust,'" *Rocky Mountain News*, January 28, 1931.
9. "U.S. Plans to Prosecute Jailed Men," *The Denver Post*, January 26, 1931.
10. "Score of North Denver Pool Halls Closed," *The Denver Post*, February 23, 1931.
11. "Mayor and Reed Rush for U.S. Aid as Public Demands Protection," *The Denver Post*, March 19, 1931.
12. "Plans to Form Bootleg Trust Nipped in Bud," *Rocky Mountain News*, January 26, 1931.
13. "Mayor and Chief Reed Were 'Tipped Off' Five Days Prior to Blast," *The Denver Post*, May 12, 1931.

## Chapter Six: Clyde

1. "Officers Drop on Roadhouse at Midnight," *Rocky Mountain News*, August 6, 1925.
2. Adeline Tate Morris, interview by Dick Kreck, July 24, 2007.
3. Ibid.
4. Robert L. Chase, "Gambling War Flares as Blast of Bomb on Starter Injures 2, Wrecks Car Parked on Grant St.," *Rocky Mountain News*, December 9, 1936.
5. Walden E. Sweet, "Denver Gangsters Bomb Two in Car," *The Denver Post*, December 9, 1936.
6. "Clyde Smaldone Put on Trial, Charged with $450 Robbery," *The Denver*

*Post*, June 16, 1937.

7. Red Fenwick, "The Smaldone Story," pt. 1, *Roundup* magazine, *The Denver Post*, December 3, 1953.

8. Gene Smaldone, interview by Dick Kreck, November 13, 2007.

9. Red Fenwick, "The Smaldone Story," pt. 3, *Roundup* magazine, *The Denver Post*, December 17, 1953.

10. Chuck Smaldone, interview by Dick Kreck and Gene Smaldone, May 3, 2007.

11. Ronnie Bay, interview by Dick Kreck and Gene Smaldone, July 16, 2007.

## CHAPTER SEVEN: CHECKERS

1. William Gallo, "The Twilight of Smaldone," *Rocky Mountain News*, October 31, 1982.

2. "Officers Blocked in Chase, Fire on Auto," *The Denver Post*, March 3, 1931.

3. Red Fenwick, "The Smaldone Story," pt. 2, *Roundup* magazine, *The Denver Post*, December 10, 1953.

4. Frederic D. Homer, *Guns and Garlic: Myths and Realities of Organized Crime* (West Lafayette, IN: Purdue Univ. Press, 1974), 130.

5. Joe Valley, interview by Dick Kreck and Gene Smaldone, June 22, 2007.

6. Ibid.

7. Ibid.

8. Chuck Smaldone, interview by Dick Kreck, April 18, 2008.

9. Ibid.

10. Pierre Wolfe, interview by Dick Kreck, August 2007.

11. Bay, interview.

12. Mike Pauldino, interview by Dick Kreck and Gene Smaldone, July 21, 2007.

13. Ibid.

14. Ibid.

15. Jerry Middleton, interview by Dick Kreck, October 5, 2007.

16. Louis Smaldone, interview by Dick Kreck and Gene Smaldone, August 10, 2007.

17. Ibid.

18. Robert Cantwell, interview by Dick Kreck, November 13, 2007.

19. Shirley Smaldone, interview by Dick Kreck and Gene Smaldone, June 1, 2007.

20. Jay Whearley, "He Didn't Look Like a Gangster," *The Denver Post*, May 12, 1974.

21. Ibid.

## CHAPTER EIGHT: PUEBLO

1. Works Project Administration, Colorado, *The WPA Guide to 1930s Colorado* (Lawrence: Univ. Press of Kansas, 1987), 182.

2. "Reputed Roma Aides Jailed When Found Heavily Armed," *The Denver Post*, June 19, 1932.
3. "Man Shot in New Gang War in Pueblo," *The Denver Post*, March 8, 1932.
4. Leonard Larsen, "Chained Between Dope Peddler, Thief," *The Denver Post*, May 5, 1953.
5. Red Fenwick, "Charley's Party Made Social (and Political) History," *The Denver Post*, January 11, 1948.
6. Valley, interview.
7. John Koncilja Jr., interview by Dick Kreck, November 1, 2007.
8. Ibid.
9. Ibid.
10. John Norton, "Former Pueblo Organized Crime Figure Dies," *Pueblo Chieftain*, February 12, 2008.

## Chapter Nine: Central City

1. William C. Russell Jr., interview by Dick Kreck, November 14, 2007.
2. "Mayor Recall Move Stirs Central City," *The Denver Post*, August 10, 1948.
3. Tom Miller, interview by Dick Kreck, December 5, 2007.
4. Russell, interview.
5. Ibid.
6. "Lid Clamped on Gambling in Central City," *The Denver Post*, July 8, 1949.
7. "Denver Gambler Named," *The Denver Post*, July 7, 1949.
8. Thor Severson, "Gaming Data 'News' to D.A.," *The Denver Post*, October 30, 1951.
9. Thor Severson, "'All News' to Enlow, Mayberry," *The Denver Post*, November 1, 1951.
10. Ibid.
11. Thor Severson, "No Smaldone Jury, Hackethal Says," *The Denver Post*, November 19, 1951.
12. Department of Regulatory Agencies, Colorado Division of Gaming, www.gaming.state.co.us/main/home.asp.

## Chapter Ten: Rich and Famous

1. John C. Polly, "30,000 Denverites Turn Out to Welcome Gov. Roosevelt, *Rocky Mountain News*, September 16, 1932.
2. "Rousing Denver Welcome Awaits Roosevelt," *Rocky Mountain News*, September 15, 1932.
3. Richard Lawrence Miller, *Truman: The Rise to Power* (New York: McGraw-Hill, 1986), 167.
4. Merle Miller, *Plain Speaking: An Oral Biography of Harry S. Truman* (New York: Berkley), 151.

5. Ibid., 196.
6. Seymour Hersh, *The Dark Side of Camelot* (New York: Little Brown, 1998), 48.
7. David G. Schwartz, *Cutting the Wire* (Reno: Univ. of Nevada Press, 2005), 3.

## Chapter Eleven: The Heights

1. Gene Smaldone, interview, November 13, 2007.
2. Valley, interview, and www.britannica.com/EBchecked/topic/52977/barbooth.
3. Denver District Attorney, *Organized Crime Report*, 1971, 49.
4. Chuck Smaldone, interview, May 3, 2007.
5. Ibid.
6. Ibid.
7. Denver Police Pension Campaign Committee, *Report of the Secretary*, May 1947.

## Chapter Twelve: 1953

1. "Feet-first Ritter under Seige," *Time* magazine, November 7, 1977.
2. "Checker's Bond Forfeited; Judge Orders Him to Stand Trial," *The Denver Post*, June 2, 1953.
3. "Testimony Describes Offers Made Juror Prospects," *The Denver Post*, October 28, 1953.
4. Bill Miller, "Government Rests Smaldone Case," *Rocky Mountain News*, October 29, 1953.
5. "Blame and Credit," editorial, *The Denver Post*, October 31, 1953.
6. Bernard Kelly, "Police Set Citywide Liquor Quiz," *The Denver Post*, November 12, 1951.
7. "Gaetano's Liquor License Application Rejected," *The Denver Post*, January 10, 1956.
8. "Geer Sued by Anthony Smaldone," *The Denver Post*, September 22, 1956.
9. Robert H. Hansen, "Smaldone Conviction Caps Brilliant Role for Outgoing Vigil," *The Denver Post*, October 30, 1953.
10. "He Knew the Answers," editorial, *The Denver Post*, October 30, 1959.
11. Bill Miller, "Smaldones Guilty!" *Rocky Mountain News*, October 30, 1953.

## Chapter Thirteen: Double-crossed

1. "A Matter of Survival," editorial, *The Denver Post*, April 1, 1955.
2. "Smaldones Given 12 Years," *The Denver Post*, August 19, 1955.
3. "Smaldones Receive 12-Year Sentences and $10,000 Fines," *Rocky Mountain News*, August 20, 1955.

4. Judgment and Commitment order, August 19, 1955, US District Court, District of Colorado, Box 102/R32, National Archives–Rocky Mountain Region, Lakewood, Colorado.
5. Robert Pattridge, "Smaldones Given 12 Years," *The Denver Post*, August 19, 1955.
6. *The Denver Post*, August 20, 1955.
7. Clyde Smaldone, letter to US District Court clerk J. Walter Bowman, January 19, 1956, Box 103/R32, National Archives–Rocky Mountain Region.
8. Peyton Ford, memorandum to Frances and Mildred Smaldone, November 30, 1956. Copy in author's collection.
9. W. M. Arnold, letter to Clyde Smaldone, February 5, 1958.
10. Bob Whearley, "'Wonderful Mother,' Mrs. Smaldone Dies," *The Denver Post*, May 2, 1962.
11. Ken Pearce, "Clyde Smaldone 'Not Mad at Anyone,'" *The Denver Post*, November 16, 1962.

## Chapter Fourteen: Chauncey, Paulie, and Eugene

1. Pauline Smaldone, interview by Dick Kreck and Gene Smaldone, May 24, 2007.
2. Ibid.
3. Ibid.
4. Shirley Smaldone, interview.
5. Bay, interview.
6. Al Ursetta, interview by Dick Kreck, September 7, 2007.
7. Barry Fey, interview by Dick Kreck, August 20, 2007.
8. Middleton, interview.
9. Jack Taylor, "Smaldones Disclaim Narcotics Connection," *The Denver Post*, March 17, 1983.

## Chapter Fifteen: The Smaldone Women

1. Gene Smaldone, interview by Dick Kreck, May 24, 2007.
2. Shirley Smaldone, interview.
3. Gene Smaldone, interview, May 24, 2007.
4. Ibid.
5. Pauline Smaldone, interview.
6. Ibid.
7. Ibid.
8. "Contract Doubted in Smaldone Shooting," *The Denver Post*, July 7, 1973.
9. "Bomb Blasts Home of Gambling Figure," *The Denver Post*, January 10, 1974.
10. Mark Thomas, "Track Ban Lifted on 'Young Gene' Smaldone," *Rocky Mountain News*, January 24, 1985.

11. Gary Gerhardt, "They'll Remember Witch Day to Observe Anniversary," *Rocky Mountain News*, August 14, 1976.

## SIDEBAR: A SECOND MOB WAR

1. Bob Whearley, "Brass Knuckle Boys Staging Comeback in Gambling Scene," *The Denver Post*, August 4, 1963.
2. Dick Prouty, "Shanks Free, Leaving State," *The Denver Post*, January 21, 1964.
3. Jerry Kennedy, interview by Dick Kreck, October 7, 2007.
4. Jay Whearley and Pat Bray, "'Skip' Lived, Died in Gangster Role," *The Denver Post*, August 5, 1973.
5. Ibid.
6. Middleton, interview.
7. Whearley and Bray, "'Skip' Lived, Died in Gangster Role."
8. Jay Whearley, "Crime Figure Slain at Lakewood Home," *The Denver Post*, July 26, 1973.

## CHAPTER SIXTEEN: RECESSIONAL

1. Pearce, "Clyde Smaldone 'Not Mad at Anyone.'"
2. Gene Smaldone, interview, November 13, 2007.
3. Ray and Mark Valente, interview by Dick Kreck and Gene Smaldone, July 2, 2007.
4. Valley, interview.
5. Ibid.
6. Jay Whearley, "He Didn't Look Like a Gangster," *The Denver Post*, May 12, 1974.
7. Ibid.
8. FBI tape, May 18, 1981, in possession of Joe Valley.
9. William Gallo, "The Twilight of Smaldone," *Rocky Mountain News*, October 31, 1982.
10. Dee Claxton, interview by Dick Kreck and Gene Smaldone, October 2, 2007.

## EPILOGUE

1. Jack Lait and Lee Mortimer, *U.S.A. Confidential* (New York: Crown, 1952).
2. Middleton, interview.
3. Horace Greeley, *An Overland Journey* (New York: Saxton, Barker, 1860).
4. Larry Britton, interview by Dick Kreck, April 20, 2007.
5. Louis Smaldone, interview.
6. Kennedy, interview.
7. Chuck Smaldone, interview, May 3, 2007.
8. Gene Smaldone, interview, November 13, 2007.
9. Claxton, interview.

# Bibliography

## Books

Alt, Betty L., and Sandra K. Wells. *Mountain Mafia: Organized Crime in the Rockies*. Nashville, TN: Cold Tree Press, 2008.

Arps, Louisa Ward. *Denver in Slices*. Athens, OH: Swallow Press, 1959.

Brenneman, Bill. *Miracle on Cherry Creek*. Denver: World Press, 1973.

Brigham, Lillian Rice. *Colorado Travelore: A Pocket Guide*. Denver: Peerless, 1938.

Casey, Lee, ed. *Denver Murders*. New York: Duell, Sloan and Pearce, 1946.

Cook, D. J. *Hands Up; Or, Twenty Years of Detective Life in the Mountains and the Plains*. Norman: Univ. of Oklahoma Press, 1958.

Cooper, Courtney Ryley. *Designs in Scarlet*. Boston: Little, Brown, 1919.

Cowley, Patricia F., and Parker M. Nielson. *The Life of Chief Judge Willis W. Ritter*. Salt Lake City: Univ. of Utah Press, 2007.

Creel, George. *Rebel at Large: Recollections of Fifty Crowded Years*. New York: Van Rees Press, 1947.

Dodds, Joanne West. *They All Came to Pueblo*. Virginia Beach, VA: Donning Co., 1994.

Downing, Sybil, and Robert E. Smith. *Tom Patterson: Colorado Crusader for Change*. Niwot, CO: Univ. Press of Colorado, 1995.

Ferrell, Robert H., ed. *Off the Record: The Private Papers of Harry S. Truman*. New York: Harper and Row, 1980.

Ferril, Thomas Hornsby. *I Hate Thursday*. New York: Harper and Bros., 1946.

Fishell, Dave. *Towers of Healing: The First 125 Years of Denver's Saint Joseph Hospital*. Denver: Saint Joseph Foundation, 1999.

Flexner, Stuart Berg. *I Hear America Talking*. New York: Van Nostrand Reinhold, 1976.

Goodstein, Phil. *The Seamy Side of Denver*. Denver: New Social Publications, 1993.

———. *The Ghosts of Denver: Capitol Hill*. Denver: New Social Publications, 1996.

———. *Robert Speer's Denver 1904–1920*. Denver: New Social Publications, 2004.

———. *In the Shadow of the Klan: When the KKK Ruled Denver 1920–1926*. Denver: New Social Publications, 2007.

————. *From Soup Lines to the Front Lines.* Denver: New Social Publications, 2007.

Granruth, Alan. *The Little Kingdom of Gilpin.* Central City, CO: Gilpin Historical Society, 2000.

Greeley, Horace. *An Overland Journey.* New York: Saxton, Barker, 1860.

Hafen, Leroy R., ed. *Colorado and Its People,* vol. II. New York: Lewis Historical Publishing, 1948.

Hayde, Frank R. *The Mafia and the Machine.* Fort Lee, NJ: Barricade, 2008.

Hersh, Seymour. *The Dark Side of Camelot.* New York: Little Brown, 1998.

Homer, Frederic D. *Guns and Garlic: Myths and Realities of Organized Crime.* West Lafayette, IN: Purdue Univ. Studies, 1974.

Hosokawa, Bill. *Thunder in the Rockies.* New York: William Morrow, 1976.

Kelly, George V. *The Old Gray Mayors of Denver.* Boulder, CO: Pruett, 1974.

Lait, Jack, and Lee Mortimer. *U.S.A. Confidential.* New York: Crown, 1952.

Leonard, Stephen J. *Lynching in Colorado 1859–1919.* Boulder, CO: Univ. Press of Colorado, 2002.

Levi, Carlo. *Christ Stopped at Eboli: The Story of a Year.* New York: Noonday Press, 1979.

Lindsey, Ben B., and Harvey J. O'Higgins. *The Beast.* New York: Doubleday, Page, 1910.

McCullough, David. *Truman.* New York: Touchstone, 1992.

Miller, Merle. *Plain Speaking: An Oral Biography of Harry S. Truman.* New York: Berkley, 1973.

Miller, Richard Lawrence. *Truman: The Rise to Power.* New York: McGraw Hill, 1986.

Noel, Thomas J. *The City and the Saloon: Denver, 1858–1916.* Niwot, CO: Univ. Press of Colorado, 1996.

————, ed. *The Glory That Was Gold.* Central City, CO: Central City Opera House Assoc., 1992.

Parkhill, Forbes, *The Wildest of the West.* New York: Henry Holt, 1957.

Perkin, Robert I. *The First Hundred Years.* New York: Doubleday, 1959.

Rolle, Andrew. *Westward the Immigrants.* Niwot, CO: Univ. Press of Colorado, 1999.

Schrager, Adam. *The Principled Politician: The Ralph Carr Story.* Golden, CO: Fulcrum, 2008.

Schlaadt, R. G. *Alcohol Use and Abuse.* Guilford, CT: Dushkin, 1992.

Schwartz, David G. *Cutting the Wire.* Reno: Univ. of Nevada Press, 2005.

Secrest, Clark. *Hell's Belles: Prostitution, Vice, and Crime in Early Denver.* Boulder, CO: University Press of Colorado, 1996.

Smiley, Jerome C. *History of Denver.* Denver: Times-Sun Publishing Co., 1901.

Student, Annette L. *Denver's Riverside Cemetery.* San Diego, CA: CSN Books, 2005.

US Treasury Department Bureau of Narcotics. *MAFIA: The Government's*

Secret File on Organized Crime. New York: Collins, 2007.

Van Cise, Philip S. Fighting the Underworld. New York: Houghton Mifflin, 1936.

Watt, Eva Hodges. Papa's Girl: The Fascinating World of Helen Bonfils. Lake City, CO: Western Reflections, 2007.

Whitmore, Julie. A History of Colorado State Penitentiary 1871–1980. Cañon City, CO: Printing Plus, 1999.

Wiberg, Ruth Eloise. Rediscovering Northwest Denver. Denver: Northwest Denver Books, 1976.

Works Progress Administration. The WPA Guide to 1930s Colorado. Lawrence: Univ. of Kansas Press, 1987 (reprint).

Wood, Richard E. Here Lies Colorado. Helena, MT: Far Country Press, 2005.

Zahller, Alisa. Italy in Colorado: Family Histories from Denver and Beyond. Virginia Beach, VA: Donning Company, 2008.

## ARTICLES, LETTERS, AND MANUSCRIPTS

Arnold, W. W., director, Kansas State Board for Vocational Education, letter to Clyde Smaldone, February 5, 1958. Copy in author's possession.

Bush, Roger. "Cooperating Individual: The True Story of Ronald A. Nocenti, An Honest Citizen Who Infiltrated the Mafia to Become a Government Informer." (Unpublished manuscript, n.d.)

National Council on Crime and Delinquency. Crooks, Crime and Colorado, 1974.

DeRose, Christine A. "Inside 'Little Italy': Italian Immigrants in Denver." Colorado Magazine 54 (June 1977).

Hansen II, James E. "A Study of Prohibition in Denver." Master's thesis, Univ. of Denver, 1965.

"Invitational Meeting," Western Thoroughbred magazine, October 1950.

Hunt, Rebecca Ann. "Urban Pioneers: Continuity and Change in the Ethnic Communities in Two Denver, Colorado, Neighborhoods 1875–1998." Dissertation, Univ. of Colorado, 1999.

Noel, Thomas J. "The Immigrant Saloon in Denver." Colorado Magazine 54 (June 1977).

Organized Crime. Report by the Organized Crime Unit Office of the District Attorney, Denver, Colorado, 1971.

Organized Crime Strike Force. State of Colorado, 1974.

Sherard, Gerald E. "Colorado Records of Arrests for Violation of Prohibition 1918–1926." Unpublished manuscript, Western History Department, Denver Public Library, 1999.

West, William Elliott. "Dry Crusade: The Prohibition Movement in Colorado, 1858–1933." PhD dissertation, Univ. of Colorado–Boulder, 1971.

## ONLINE

Digital History, "Italian Immigration." www.digitalhistory.uh.edu/history online/Italian_immigration.cfm.

Geocities. "The Colorado LCN Family: The Early Years (1900s–1933)." www .geocities.com/OrganizedCrimeSyndicates/colorado.html.

Historical Documents. "The Volstead Act, October 28, 1919." www.historical documents.com/VolsteadAct.htm.

Johnson, Scott, and Craig Johnson. "Who Were the Famous Blonger Brothers?" www.blongerbros.com.

Leavenworth Convention and Visitors Bureau. "Area Prison Information." www.lvarea.com.

Machi, Mario, Allan May, and Charlie Molino. "Denver Crime Family." www .americanmafia.com/Cities/Denver.html.

ThinkQuest. "Immigration: The Journey to America: The Italians." http:// library.thinkquest.org/20619/Italian.html.

## LIBRARIES

Western History and Genealogy Department, Denver Public Library; Colorado Historical Society, Denver, CO; National Archives–Rocky Mountain Region, Lakewood, CO; Clerk's office, US District Court, Denver; Museum of Colorado Prisons, Cañon City , CO; City-County Library, Pueblo, CO.

## INTERVIEWS

Taped interviews with the following persons, conducted in 2007, are in the oral history collection of the Western History and Genealogy Department of the Denver Public Library:

Chuck Smaldone, April 13, 2007, and May 3, 2007
Larry Britton, retired Denver Police captain, April 20, 2007
Gene Smaldone, May 23, 2007, and November 13, 2007
Pauline Smaldone, May 24, 2007
Shirley Smaldone, June 1, 2007
Joe Valley, June 22, 2007
Excerpts of FBI eavesdrop tapes (in possession of Joe Valley in 2009)
Ray Longo, June 29, 2007
Ben Dreith, July 2, 2007
Ray and Mark Valente, July 2, 2007
Ronnie Bay, July 16, 2007
Mike Pauldino, July 21, 2007
Adeline Tate Morris, July 24, 2007
Pierre Wolfe, August 2007
Percy Conro, August 2007
Louis Smaldone, August 10, 2007

Barry Fey, August 20, 2007
Al Ursetta, September 7, 2007
John "Bug Dust" Madonna, October 1, 2007
Eddie Domenico, October 1, 2007
Fred Tesone, October 1, 2007
Dee Claxton, October 2, 2007
Jerry Middleton, October 5, 2007
Jerry Kennedy, retired Denver Police captain, October 7, 2007
John Koncilja Jr., Investigator, Pueblo District Attorney, retired Pueblo PD, November 1, 2007
Robert Cantwell, head of CBI, former Denver cop, November 13, 2007
William C. Russell Jr., November 14, 2007
Ray Imel Jr., December 5, 2007
Tom Miller, December 5, 2007

## NEWSPAPERS AND MAGAZINES

*The Denver Post*
*The Denver Times*
*The Pueblo Chieftain*
*Rocky Mountain News*
*Time* magazine

# INDEX